Basic Skills for the
TOEFL® iBT

Moraig Macgillivray
Kayang Gagiano

Compass
Publishing

Reading 3

Basic Skills for the TOEFL® iBT 3
Reading

Kayang Gagiano · Moraig Macgillivray

© 2008 Compass Publishing

Project Editor: Liana Robinson
Acquisitions Editor: Emily Page
Content Editor: Alexander Page
Copy Editor: Alice Wrigglesworth
Consultants: Lucy Han, Chanhee Park
Cover/Interior Design: Dammora Inc

email: info@compasspub.com
http://www.compasspub.com

ISBN: 978-1-59966-161-2

10 9 8 7 6 5 4 3
12 11 10 09

Contents

Introduction to the TOEFL® iBT

What is the TOEFL® test?

The TOEFL® iBT test (Test of English as a Foreign Language Internet-based test) is designed to assess English proficiency in non-native speakers who want to achieve academic success as well as effective communication. It is not meant to test academic knowledge or computer ability; therefore, questions are always based on material found in the test.

The TOEFL® iBT test is divided into four sections:
- Reading
- Listening
- Speaking
- Writing

TOEFL® Scores

TOEFL® scores can be used for:
- Admission into university or college where instruction is in English
- Employers or government agencies who need to determine a person's English ability
- English-learning institutes which need to place students in the appropriate level of English instruction

It is estimated that about 4,400 universities and other institutions require a certain TOEFL® test score for admission.

The exact calculation of a TOEFL® test score is complicated and not necessary for the student to understand. However, it is helpful to know that:
- Each section in the Internet-based test is worth 30 points
- The highest possible score on the iBT is 120 points
- Each institution will have its own specific score requirements

✻ It is very important to check with each institution individually to find out what its admission requirements are.

Registering for the TOEFL® iBT

Students who wish to take the TOEFL® test must get registration information. Registration information can be obtained online at the ETS website. The Internet address is www.ets.org/toefl.

The website provides information such as:
- testing locations
- costs
- identification requirements
- other test preparation material
- registration information
- test center locations

This information will vary depending on the country in which you take the test. Be sure to follow the requirements carefully. If you do not have the proper requirements in order, you may not be able to take the test. Remember that if you register online, you will need to have your credit card information ready.

Introduction to the Reading Section of the TOEFL® iBT

In the reading section of the TOEFL® test, you will be required to read 3-5 passages on varying topics. After each passage, you will answer 12-14 questions that test your ability to:
- understand vocabulary
- recognize sentence structure
- determine factual information
- determine implied information
- recognize the writer's intention

You will not be permitted to see the questions until after you have read the passage. While answering the questions, you will be permitted to look back at the reading. You do not need any previous knowledge on the topic in order to answer the questions correctly.

Passage Types:

1. Exposition—material that provides information about or an explanation of a topic
2. Argumentation—material that presents a point of view about a topic and provides supporting evidence in favor of a position
3. Narrative—an account of a person's life or a historical event

Reading Question Types:

Most questions will be multiple-choice questions. The following list explains the types and number of each type of question per passage. Questions may not appear in this order.

Question Type	Number	Description
Vocabulary	3-4	Choose the best meaning of a word or phrase
Reference	0-1	Identify the noun to which a pronoun is referring
Factual Information	2-4	Select details or facts provided in the passage
Negative Fact	1	Identify details or facts NOT provided, or NOT true according to the passage
Sentence Simplification	1	Choose the best answer to demonstrate your understanding of a sentence and your ability to analyze its meaning
Inference	0-1	Draw an inference from the passage by choosing an answer that is not actually said in the passage, but is implied or can be inferred
Rhetorical Purpose	1-2	Identify why the writer has mentioned something in a certain way or in a certain place
Insert Text	1	Insert a sentence into the most appropriate place in the passage
Summary	0-1	Choose the sentences that best summarize the entire passage
Table	0-1	Categorize major ideas or important information from the passage

Most questions are worth 1 point each, however Summary questions are worth 2 points and Table questions are worth 3-4 points.

Test management

- Questions cannot be viewed until after the passage has been read.

- You can return to previous questions you may wish to revise or recheck by using the Review icon at the top of the screen.

- You will be allowed to study the reading as you attempt the questions.

- There is a glossary included for some words.

- When reading passages, ask yourself the following important questions:
    - ⇨ What is the main idea of the passage?
    - ⇨ How is the main idea developed/supported in the passage?
    - ⇨ What is the main point/role of each paragraph?

- You have 60-100 minutes to read the passages and answer 12-14 questions per passage. This usually means approximately 20 minutes per passage and set of questions. Try to pace yourself accordingly. The recommended reading speed would be approximately 100-150 words per minute. Therefore, you should try to read the passages in this book at that speed.

- For each set of questions, first answer all of the questions that you can answer easily. You can then go back and answer questions that are more difficult if you have time.

[01] History

Getting Ready to Read

A. Learn the words.

Key Vocabulary

acceptable	approved; allowed; thought to be OK
battle	an instance of armed conflict between opposing armies
equal	having the same capabilities and worth
dainty	delicate
frail	weak; easily damaged

TOEFL® Vocabulary

forbidden	not allowed
risk	potential harm
conform	to adhere to standards
oppose	to be against
undergo	to endure

B. Learn the question types.

TOEFL® Question Types

Vocabulary

The word X in the passage is closest in meaning to . . .

In stating X, the author means that . . .

- Incorrect answer choices may contain synonyms to words found near the word in question.
- Incorrect answer choices may contain correct meanings of the word if it were used in a different context.

Reference

The word X in the passage refers to . . .

The phrase X in paragraph Y refers to . . .

- Incorrect answer choices might include nouns and phrases found in the passage but are not referred to by the referent in question.
- Incorrect answer choices will not make sense when substituted in for the referent in question.

C. Read the passage. Number each paragraph with the correct main idea or purpose.

> 1. Information on the history of women's status in America
> 2. An example of an early woman's contribution to the military
> 3. Information on why some people are against women fighting
> 4. General history of women in the military

Women in the Military

___ Today, many women serve in the military. However, this was not always acceptable. Women used to be forbidden from fighting in battles. However, some women felt strongly about fighting. They dressed up as men so they could fight.

___ The first woman to serve in the American military did so in 1782. However, she served under the name Robert Shurtliff. Her real name was Deborah Sampson and her secret was discovered by a doctor when she was shot in the leg.

___ Women have worked hard for many years to be seen as equals. Militaries, however, still don't like women to fight because of the risk. Historically, men have often made laws to protect women. However, many women do not conform to people's ideas of how they should act. For example, many are not dainty and frail.

___ Many people are opposed to the idea of women fighting. They say that women are not as strong as men are. They say that women could put others in danger. Others say that some women are strong enough. They can undergo the same training as men. Therefore, they should be allowed to fight like men.

D. Complete the summary notes by filling in the blanks.

Topic:	_____
General history:	Today — OK for women to serve _____. Women used to be _____.
Example:	The _____ in the American military was Deborah Sampson in _____. Pretended to be _____. Was discovered by a _____.
Women's status:	Women have worked hard to be seen as _____. Militaries don't want women to fight because _____. Laws were often made to _____. Not all women conform to _____.
Opposition:	Some think that women are physically _____. Others say that some women are _____. Standards should be the _____.

E. Choose the correct answers.

1. The word forbidden is closest in meaning to

(A) prohibited   (B) permitted

2. The word risk is closest in meaning to

(A) danger   (B) chance

3. The phrase her secret in the passage refers to

(A) her wound   (B) her gender

4. The word many in the passage refers to

(A) women   (B) men

TOEFL® Vocabulary Practice

F. Fill in the blanks with the correct words.

| forbidden | risk | conform | opposed | undergo |

1. Many young adults of the 1960s refused to _____ to societal norms.

2. The flight was delayed because of a high security _____.

3. He had to _____ radiation therapy for his cancer.

4. She is _____ to legalized gambling because she believes it is a sin.

5. Plagiarism is _____ and you will be expelled if you are caught.

Practice

A. Learn the words.

tribe	a group of people who live together and who share culture and traditions
settler	one who settles or makes a home in a new place
treaty	a contract or agreement
dependent	the condition of relying on another for survival
collapse	to decline sharply

exploit	to use to one's own advantage; to overwork
labor	work, often physical
integrity	moral character
displace	to cause to become dispersed; to force to leave
expose	to come into contact with

Reading Passage

B. Read the passage and underline the key information.

Native Americans

Europeans settled in the region now known as the United States starting in the sixteenth century. But the land was not empty when they arrived. There were already people living there. They were the Native Americans. They lived in groups called tribes. Most of them worked doing physical labor. Some moved from place to place hunting. Others stayed in one place and farmed. They did not exploit the land. They took only what they needed. The outlook of the white settlers contradicted that of the natives. They saw the land as a possession. They were very wasteful.

White settlers did not see the Natives as people. They did not respect the integrity of their culture. Instead, they took over their land. They displaced groups of Native Americans. They also fought with them and spread diseases to them. The arrival of white settlers resulted in a population collapse among the Native peoples.

The spread of disease was significant. White people introduced diseases that the natives had never been exposed to before. This made it harder for them to fight the diseases. It is guessed that up to eighty percent of native populations were killed by disease.

Those who survived had to live with the white settlers. Treaties were created to settle land claims. Native groups gave up many rights in these treaties. In exchange, the government made certain promises. This made the natives highly dependent of the government. Many natives opposed these treaties. When groups chose not to enter into a treaty, they were forced to leave the land anyway.

C. Choose the correct answers.

1. The word them in the passage refers to

(A) tribes   (B) Native Americans

2. The word fight in the passage is closest in meaning to

(A) argue   (B) combat

3. Which of the following is true of Native American tribes prior to the arrival of Europeans?

(A) They had no diseases.   (B) They valued natural resources.

4. Why did most Native Americans die following the arrival of Europeans?

(A) Because they got sick   (B) Because they were killed in battles

TOEFL® Vocabulary Practice

D. Fill in the blanks with the correct words.

exploited	labor	integrity	displaced	expose

1. Working on a building site often requires hard _____.

2. Responsible consumers do not buy products that were produced in sweatshops where children and other workers are _____.

3. You shouldn't _____ your skin to UV rays, as they can cause cancer. Always cover up with light clothes or wear sunscreen.

4. Thousands of people lost their homes and were _____ as a result of the war and are now refugees in a neighboring country.

5. The scandal was especially shocking because he was thought to be a man of _____.

Read the passage.

Child Labor

Throughout most of human history, children have worked. They have always helped out at home. Even children in early human societies worked. They helped their mothers gather fruit and berries. When people started farming, children helped their families by working on the farm. But the Industrial Revolution changed the nature of child labor.

The Industrial Revolution saw the rise of factories. Goods were now mass-produced. There was no need for skilled craftsmen. ■ 1) The owners of factories wanted to make as much money as they could. The best way to do that was to pay low wages. Children were easily exploited. Some had poor parents. Others had lost their parents. ■ 2) They needed to earn a wage. But they had no power to demand high wages. As a result, factory owners paid children very little. ■ 3) These young people sometimes worked sixteen hours per day. Clearly, they could not attend school. As such, they couldn't hope for a better life when they grew up. ■ 4) Work conditions were also unsafe. Children risked their lives to earn a wage. The factories were dark. They did not conform to the safety standards we have today. Many children therefore died or were seriously hurt while working.

There were many people who opposed the practice of employing children. They believed that it was wrong to subject children to such a life. They began a social movement. It was aimed at creating laws to protect children from exploitation at work. In time, laws were made to protect children in the workforce. For starters, it was forbidden to make children work too much. Safety standards were made. In time, the demand for an educated workforce increased. So it was important to increase the number of educated people. Sending children to work instead of to school contradicted this aim. As such, mandatory universal education was established. That meant that all children had to go to school until age sixteen. So, they did not have a lot of time for factory work. Today, children generally can't work until they are sixteen.

Choose the correct answers.

1. The word nature in the passage is closest in meaning to
   - (A) character
   - (B) scenery
   - (C) environment
   - (D) custom

2. All of the following were mentioned as characteristics of child labor EXCEPT
   - (A) long hours
   - (B) dangerous environment
   - (C) frequent beatings
   - (D) low wages

3. The word they in the passage refers to
   (A) parents   (B) children
   (C) factory owners   (D) workers

4. Which of the following can be inferred about improvements in child labor?

   (A) That they were mainly the result of public outcry.
   (B) That they were mainly the result of the changing nature of the economy.
   (C) That they were mainly the result of a surplus in adult workers.
   (D) That they were mainly the result of improved technology.

5. Look at the four squares (■) that indicate where the following sentence could be added to the passage.

They also subjected them to harsh conditions.

   (A) Square 1   (B) Square 2
   (C) Square 3   (D) Square 4

6. An introductory sentence for a brief summary of the passage is provided below. Complete the summary by selecting the THREE answer choices that express the most important ideas in the passage. Some sentences do not belong in the summary because they express ideas that are not presented in the passage or are minor ideas in the passage.

Child labor became problematic during the Industrial Revolution.

   (A) Children became easily exploited by factory owners.
   (B) They had to give up their handicrafts and go to work in factories.
   (C) They worked long hours in unsafe conditions for little pay.
   (D) Laws were passed limiting the number of hours children could work, making age restrictions, and requiring school.
   (E) When children turn sixteen they can leave school and go to work in factories, but not before.
   (F) Factory owners demanded government controls so that they could continue to make a profit without exploiting children.

Check-up

A. Choose the correct answers.

1. When answering a vocabulary question, you should

    (A) eliminate answer choices that contain synonyms of words near the word in question.

    (B) choose the answer choice that contains an antonym of the word in question.

    (C) eliminate answer choices that contain a synonym of the word in question.

    (D) choose the answer choice that contains the opposite meaning of the word in question.

2. What should you do when answering a reference question?

    (A) Choose the answer choice that contains words or phrases not related to the referent.

    (B) Eliminate answer choices that contain words or phrases near the referent but not related to it.

    (C) Choose the answer choice that doesn't make sense when substituted for the referent.

    (D) Eliminate answer choices that make sense when substituted in for the referent.

Key Vocabulary Practice

B. Fill in the blanks with the correct words.

acceptable	battle	equal	dainty	frail
tribe	settlers	treaty	dependent	collapse

1. The two candidates are _____ in their credentials, but one has more experience.

2. Most comic books feature a(n) _____ between a superhero and an evil villain.

3. It is not a good time to sell because of the recent _____ in housing prices.

4. He is getting _____ in his old age. If he falls he could easily break his hip.

5. The _____ had to clear the land of trees and shrubs before they could build their homes.

6. She was not a(n) _____ little girl. She liked to play rough with the boys.

7. Certain behaviors that are _____ in one country might be considered rude in another.

8. The two leaders signed the _____ to make the agreement legal.

9. He belonged to a(n) _____ that moved around in search of food.

10. Children are _____ on their parents for food and shelter until they are old enough to work.

[02] Visual Arts

Getting Ready to Read

A. Learn the words.

Key Vocabulary

photography	the art of taking photographs
subject	a person, place, or thing featured in a piece of art
expose	to subject to light
sharp	clearly defined
frame	a border used for a picture

TOEFL® Vocabulary

enormous	very big
infer	to come to an understanding through reason and logic
attach	to connect to
insert	to put inside
precede	to come before

B. Learn the question types.

TOEFL® Question Types

Factual Information

The author's description of X mentions which of the following?

According to the passage, X occurred because

According to the author, X did Y because

- Incorrect answer choices may repeat unrelated details from the passage.
- Incorrect answer choices may include information not mentioned in the passage.

Negative Factual Information

According to the passage, which of the following is NOT true of X?

The author's description of X mentions all of the following EXCEPT.

- Incorrect answer choices include details that are directly stated in the passage.
- Correct answer choices may include details that are directly stated in the passage but not in connection to the topic of the question.

C. Read the passage. Number each paragraph with the correct main idea or purpose.

1. A summary sentence of the passage
2. Information about the ambrotype
3. Information about the tintype
4. Information about the daguerreotype
5. An introduction to 19th century photography

Nineteenth Century Photography

___ The nineteenth century saw enormous advances in photography in the US. Photos from this time period can tell us about history. But they don't just tell us about the subject of the photo. We can learn about the art of photography.

___ We can infer the date of a photo by the style. The daguerreotype, for example, was the earliest style in common use. A silver-plated, mirror-like metal sheet was used. It was placed in a camera and exposed to the image. The final image was sharp and full of detail.

___ The ambrotype was used from 1854 to the early 1860s. It became popular because it was cheaper than the daguerreotype. It used a glass plate to expose the image in the camera. Another glass plate was then attached to protect it. Then the whole thing was inserted into a metal frame.

___ The ambrotype preceded the tintype. The tintype used a thin, black, metal plate instead of glass. It was invented in 1856. It was popular until the early 1900s. The photos didn't have to be cased like ambrotypes. This was because they weren't so fragile.

___ These are just a few of the many techniques used in photography in America in the nineteenth century.

D. Complete the summary notes by filling in the blanks.

Topic:	_____
Introduction:	Nineteenth century photography in the US saw _____ _____. We can learn about _____. We can learn about the art of _____.
Daguerreotype:	Used a _____ sheet, like a _____. Exposed to image from inside the _____. Final image was _____.
Ambrotype:	Used from _____ to _____. Popular because it was _____. Used one _____ to expose image and another to _____. Final image inserted into a _____.
Tintype:	Used a thin, black, _____. Invented in _____ and popular until _____. Weren't as _____ as ambrotypes.

E. Choose the correct answers.

1. According to the passage, what were daguerreotype photos like?

(A) blurry   (B) sharp

2. According to the passage, what kind of plate was used in ambrotype photography?

(A) glass   (B) metal

3. Which of the following was NOT mentioned as a material used in plates?

(A) metal   (B) paper

4. Which of the following is NOT true, according to the passage?

(A) The daguerreotype was the cheapest style.

(B) The ambrotype was the most fragile style.

TOEFL® Vocabulary Practice

F. Fill in the blanks with the correct words.

enormous	infer	attached	insert	precedes

1. The national anthem always _____ the game.

2. The elephant looked _____ next to the puppy.

3. Even though he didn't confess, we can _____ from the evidence that he is guilty.

4. After you _____ the disk into the disk drive, it should start to load automatically.

5. I _____ a note to the file to remind her to call the client.

Practice

A. Learn the words.

Key Vocabulary

liberty	freedom; independence from rule
flee	to run away
oppress	to use authority to subject another to unjust conditions
visual	relating to things we can see
shackles	a device used to prevent escape

TOEFL® Vocabulary

adjacent	beside; next to
scenario	situation
diversity	the state of having many different types; variety
invoke	to bring about; to cause
found	to establish

Reading Passage

B. Read the passage and underline the key information.

The Statue of Liberty

The Statue of Liberty is one of the most famous statues in the world. It stands on Liberty Island which is in New York Harbor. It was a gift to the United States from France in 1886. The reason for the gift was the hundredth birthday of the US. The statue wasn't actually dedicated until ten years later, though. It was meant as a gesture of friendship.

Ellis Island lies adjacent to the statue. It is known as the Gateway to America. Before flying became common, people arrived in America from Europe in boats. Ellis Island was a common landing spot for these boats. The people arriving were often fleeing scenarios where they were oppressed. They saw the Statue of Liberty when they arrived. It stood as a visual symbol of their new found freedom and liberty.

This freedom and liberty is represented in the statue. The woman is stepping forward. The shackles that had bound her feet are broken. This is symbolic. It is a symbol of the United States breaking free and becoming a nation. This is shown in the tablet. The woman carries a tablet that says July 4, 1776. That was the day the US became an independent country.

America is a nation rich with diversity. This is because it was founded by immigrants. These immigrants came from many different places. Furthermore, it has been a destination for people from all over the world. The reason is that it is a free nation. Therefore, for Americans, the Statue of Liberty invokes feelings of national pride.

C. Choose the correct answers.

1. Why did France give the Statue of Liberty to the US?

(A) To commemorate a hundred years of independence

(B) Because it represented freedom and democracy

2. The word bound in the passage is closest in meaning to

(A) destined   (B) confined

3. Which of the following is NOT true of the Statue of Liberty?

(A) It's on Ellis Island.   (B) It features a tablet.

4. The word that in the passage refers to

(A) the tablet   (B) the date

TOEFL® Vocabulary Practice

D. Fill in the blanks with the correct words.

adjacent	scenarios	diversity	invoke	founded

1. This city was _____ in 1749.

2. The speech was meant to _____ a sense of pride.

3. Reality shows place regular people in different _____ so that audiences can watch how they behave.

4. The parking lot lies _____ to the building.

5. Some people want to limit immigration, but I prefer to live in a place with a lot of _____.

Test

Read the passage.

Visual Arts

Visual arts are arts that appeal to our sense of sight. As such, the possibilities for visual arts are endless. Paintings, drawings, film, and sculptures are just a few examples. There has been some disagreement as to what should be included in the visual arts. Namely, should crafts be seen as such? There was a time when only fine arts could be included in the visual arts. Craftsmen were not thought to be artists. This era preceded the Arts and Crafts Movement which was founded in the early twentieth century. This movement helped create an appreciation for craftsmanship. Today, crafts too are considered visual arts.

Our ideas of what constitutes art are always changing. ■ 1) A modern example is graffiti. ■ 2) Graffiti is seen by some as vandalism. ■ 3) They think it is ugly. ■ 4) But others see it as art. For one thing, it can be very beautiful. For another, it can make a strong statement about society.

The visual arts are as old as humanity. Some of the earliest examples of visual arts are cave paintings. These were made by early humans. They would often depict scenarios such as hunting. Such paintings not only tell us about the daily lives of these early humans, but they tell us something about their psyches. In other words, we can see what their lives were like, but we can infer something about the way their minds worked. For example, some cave paintings indicate that the artists held religious beliefs.

A good visual artist does more than depict an image. He or she attaches meaning to that image. The hope is that it will invoke a certain emotional response in the viewer. The range of possible responses, of course, is enormous. Again, the work can tell us much about the subject. But it can tell us even more about the artist.

There is a great diversity in the types of visual art available. And the possibilities are growing. New technologies allow for new genres. Computer graphics, for example, has opened up a world of possibilities to artists. And the quality gets better and better as technology improves.

Choose the correct answers.

1. What is the most recent example of visual arts mentioned in the passage?

(A) cave paintings   (B) film

(C) computer graphics   (D) sculptures

2. The word these in the passage refers to

(A) visual arts   (B) examples

(C) cave paintings   (D) early humans

3. The word work in the passage is closest in meaning to

(A) labor
(B) job
(C) business
(D) piece

4. Which of the following was NOT mentioned in reference to visual art?

(A) early humans
(B) graphic novels
(C) technology
(D) vandalism

5. Look at the four squares (■) that indicate where the following sentence could be added to the passage.

And there is often a lot of disagreement.

Where would the sentence best fit?

(A) Square 1
(B) Square 2
(C) Square 3
(D) Square 4

6. Directions: Complete the table by choosing whether each art genre is visual art or another type of art. TWO of the answer choices will not be used.
This question is worth 3 points.

(A) Music
(B) Chess
(C) Tennis
(D) Photography
(E) Computer graphics
(F) Sculpture
(G) Literature

Visual Art
- _____
- _____
- _____

Other Art
- _____
- _____

Check-up

A. Choose the correct answers.

1. When answering a factual information question, you should
   (A) eliminate answer choices that include details mentioned directly in the passage.
   (B) choose the answer choice with details unrelated to the passage.
   (C) eliminate answer choices that repeat details from the passage that are not related to the question.
   (D) choose the answer choice with details from the passage that are not related to the question.

2. What should you do when answering a negative factual information question?
   (A) Eliminate answer choices opposite to those mentioned directly in the passage.
   (B) Eliminate answer choices that include details mentioned directly in the passage.
   (C) Eliminate answer choices that contradict the information in the passage.
   (D) Eliminate answer choices that include information not mentioned in the passage.

Key Vocabulary Practice

B. Fill in the blanks with the correct words.

photography	subject	expose	sharp	frame
liberty	fled	oppressed	visual	shackles

1. The inmates are kept in _____ so they can't escape.
2. I love taking pictures. I think I'll join a(n) _____ group.
3. The people were tired of being _____ by an evil dictator.
4. The artist really captured the inner turmoil of the _____.
5. The robbers _____ the scene when they heard police sirens.
6. This picture is blurry. We can use a computer program to make it _____.
7. You must be careful not to _____ the film until you get in the dark room.
8. A(n) _____ advertisement uses a picture to get the customer's attention.
9. The United States is known as the land of _____.
10. That's a nice photo. You should put it in a(n) _____ and hang it up.

[03] Life Sciences

Getting Ready to Read

A. Learn the words.

Key Vocabulary

microscope	instrument that magnifies size, used for looking at small objects
micro organism	the smallest living things, too small to see with the naked eye
scientific	having to do with science or the sciences
philosopher	a thinker; someone concerned with the nature of the universe
experiment	a trial; something done to test a theory

TOEFL® Vocabulary

biology	the study of living things
accurate	precise; to be sure something is correct
perseverance	a skill to keep doing things even if they are difficult
rigorous	rigidly strict and exact; sticking to the rules
confine	to limit, trap or imprison; to create a boundary

B. Learn the question types.

TOEFL® Question Types

Sentence Simplification
Which of the following best expresses the essential information in the highlighted sentence? *Incorrect* answers change the meaning in important ways or leave out essential information.

- Incorrect answer choices may contain important details from the highlighted sentence but use them differently.
- Incorrect answer choices may contradict the message of the highlighted sentence.

C. Read the passage. Number each paragraph with the correct main idea or purpose.

1. Information about the "father of biology"
2. What "biology" means
3. Information on Aristotle's beliefs
4. What Life Science is about
5. Information on Aristotle's methods

Life Science

___ Life Science is the study of all living things. It is the study of animals, humans, and plants. It is also the study of tiny living things that can only be seen with a microscope. We call these small things micro-organisms.

___ Life Science is also sometimes called biology. This word comes from two Greek words: "bio," meaning "life" and "logos," meaning "to speak of." Many scientific words come from Greek. This is because the ancient Greeks were some of the first people to try and understand nature. They wrote their ideas down and today we can still read them.

___ Aristotle, a Greek philosopher, who lived from 384 BCE until 322 BCE, is known as the "father of biology." He was one of the very first people to make highly accurate studies of animals and plants.

___ Aristotle had a lot of perseverance. He knew that he had to study the same animal or plant for a long time to get to know it. He studied living things carefully. He also did many experiments. He wrote down everything he saw.

___ Aristotle believed that all scientists had to be rigorous and that they could not guess. That is also why he did not confine his studies to one place. He traveled a lot. Today, life scientists still use many of his methods.

D. Complete the summary notes by filling in the blanks.

Topic:	_____
What it is:	The study of all _____: animals, _____, and plants. Also of _____.
Other name:	_____, comes from _____. Many _____ words are Greek because they studied _____.
Aristotle:	Greek _____, lived _____. Known as _____. One of _____ people to make very _____ studies of _____.
His methods:	Had a lot of _____. Studied each animal for a long _____ to get to _____.
His beliefs:	Scientists have to be _____, can't take _____. Didn't _____ his studies. He _____ a lot. Many of his _____ still used today.

E. Choose the correct answers.

1. Which of the following best expresses the essential information in the first highlighted sentence? Incorrect answers change the meaning in important ways or leave out essential information.

   He was one of the very first people to make highly accurate studies of animals and plants.

   (A) He was one of the only men who ever studied living things very carefully.
   (B) He was a pioneer who observed nature in detail and always wanted to be precise.

2. The word philosopher in paragraph 3 is closest in meaning to

   (A) scientist   (B) thinker

3. Which of the following best expresses the essential information in the second highlighted sentence? Incorrect answers change the meaning in important ways or leave out essential information.

   Aristotle believed that all scientists had to be rigorous and that they could not guess.

   (A) Aristotle thought that scientists should be strict and not take chances.
   (B) Aristotle imagined that scientists could be great, as long as they took risks.

4. According to the passage, which of the following is NOT true of Aristotle?

   (A) He didn't like to travel.   (B) He did a lot of experiments.

F. Fill in the blanks with the correct words.

confined	perseverance	biology	accurate	rigorous

1. _____ exercise can harm your health, so moderate exercise is better.

2. During national elections it is very important that vote counts are _____.

3. Marine _____ is the scientific study of sea life.

4. Olympic athletes need a lot of _____ and practice to win gold medals.

5. Queen Elizabeth I had her enemies _____ in the Tower of London.

Practice

A. Learn the words.

Key Vocabulary

origin	the place something comes from or develops from
species	a group of living things with the same qualities and characteristics
Bible	a religious work with stories, psalms and teachings for Judaism and Christianity
evil	wicked; bad; something which does great harm; malicious
ignore	to give no attention to something; to pretend something does not exist

TOEFL® Vocabulary

controversial	generating debate and argument; causing a war of opinions
evolution	process of development or change over time
colleague	someone you work with
incompatible	cannot function or exist together in harmony
prohibit	to prevent, disallow or stop something

Reading Passage

B. Read the passage and underline the key information.

Evolution

In 1859, a man called Charles Darwin wrote a famous but controversial book. The book was called *On the Origin of Species*. It was about something called "evolution." This was a very exciting idea about how animals and plants changed over millions of years.

Darwin had traveled all over the world. He had studied many different plants and animals. He could see how they all adapted to their environments. He saw that animals that lived in deserts did not use a lot of water. He saw that animals that lived in the snow had thick fur to keep them warm. He decided that it took a long time for animals and plants to change like this. He thought it took thousands of years for them to change just a little.

Darwin believed that people had also changed over time. He wrote that people and monkeys had come from the same animal. He had a colleague called Thomas Huxley who also thought so. They upset many people. The idea was incompatible with the Bible. The Bible said that God had made people.

The church tried to prohibit students from learning about evolution. They thought Darwin's ideas were evil. There was a lot of evidence to show that Darwin was right and his ideas could not be ignored.

Darwin also saw how weaker animals often died while stronger animals didn't. This meant that only the strongest and smartest animals would have babies. Darwin thought this was nature's way of making sure that there would only be strong animals on Earth.

C. Choose the correct answers.

1. Which of the following best expresses the essential information in the first highlighted sentence? Incorrect answers change the meaning in important ways or leave out essential information.

This was a very exciting idea about how animals and plants changed over millions of years.

(A) This was the unusual proposal that living things never develop over time.

(B) This was a refreshing concept that flora and fauna adapted over millennia.

2. According to the passage, Darwin upset many people because
(A) he said people and monkeys came from the same animal
(B) he did not believe in God

3. Which of the following best expresses the essential information in the second highlighted sentence? Incorrect answers change the meaning in important ways or leave out essential information.

There was a lot of evidence to show that Darwin was right and his ideas could not be ignored.

(A) There was much proof that Darwin was correct and that people should give his theory attention.

(B) There was a great deal of arguing for Darwin's rights and his thoughts were widely supported.

4. The word prohibit in paragraph 4 is closest in meaning to
(A) allow   (B) disallow

D. Fill in the blanks with the correct words.

colleagues	evolution	incompatible	controversial	prohibit

1. Laws that _____ smoking in public places are found in most countries.

2. The decision to impeach President Bill Clinton in 1999 was a(n) _____ one.

3. The _____ of computer technology has been very rapid.

4. Marie Curie and her husband, Pierre, were _____ who worked well together.

5. When husbands and wives are _____, marriages often end in divorce.

Test

Read the passage.

Germs

How and why do people get sick? This is something no one could understand for thousands of years. Through all the stages of evolution people had to fight disease. Diseases are caused by tiny micro-organisms called germs.

Germs cannot be ignored because they are part of the living world. Long ago, before scientists knew what germs were, philosophers thought evil spirits made people sick. Others thought that God made you sick if you did something wrong. The Bible was filled with stories about people getting ill because they had done bad things.

People did not really know anything about germs until the nineteenth century. It was only through the perseverance of a few scientists that we found out about them. In 1860, a French scientist called Louis Pasteur did many experiments to learn about germs. He was very rigorous and this took him a long time. He had to work very hard and he did not have any colleagues to help him. Pasteur knew that he had to be accurate before he told the world what he had found. He knew that many doctors would find his information about germs controversial. Pasteur's findings were incompatible with the beliefs of many doctors of that time. Pasteur found out that diseases are spread by germs. The germs were even found on doctor's medical tools. ■ 1) Pasteur told the doctors they had to boil their tools in water to kill the germs. ■ 2) He also told them that they had to wash their hands well after working with sick people. ■ 3) If they did not, they would spread disease to others. ■ 4)

Pasteur also found out that by heating liquids, one could kill germs. He heated liquids like milk and wine and killed all the germs. From that time on, it was safe to drink them. These days, governments usually prohibit the sale of milk or wine that has not been heated in this way.

Choose the correct answers.

1. The word micro-organism in paragraph 1 is closest in meaning to
   (A) small living thing
   (B) large living thing
   (C) small harmful thing
   (D) large harmful thing

2. The word they at the end of paragraph 2 refers to
   (A) scientists
   (B) people
   (C) germs
   (D) philosophers

3. According to the passage which of the following is NOT true of Louis Pasteur?

(A) He was very rigorous and did many experiments.
(B) His findings were incompatible with many doctor's beliefs.
(C) He had many colleagues to help him.
(D) He told doctors to boil their medical tools.

4. Which of the following best expresses the essential information in the highlighted sentence? Incorrect answers change the meaning in important ways or leave out essential information.

He also told them that they had to wash their hands well after working with sick people.

(A) He didn't tell them to be clean because he knew it would not help sick patients.
(B) He also asked them to wash their tools carefully after being near the sick.
(C) He insisted that they rub their hands well before helping diseased people.
(D) In addition, he asked that they cleanse their hands properly after handling ill patients.

5. Look at the four squares (■) that indicate where the following sentence could be added to the passage.

Pasteur saved many lives in this way.

Where would the sentence best fit?

(A) Square 1   (B) Square 2
(C) Square 3   (D) Square 4

6. Directions: An introductory sentence for a brief summary of the passage is provided below. Complete the summary by selecting the THREE answer choices that express the most important ideas in the passage. Some sentences do not belong in the summary because they express ideas that are not presented in the passage or are minor ideas in the passage.

The scientific history of germs is very interesting.

(A) In the nineteenth century we finally learned about germs through the perseverance and experiments of scientists like Louis Pasteur.
(B) Louis Pasteur had no one to help him and so he had to work very hard doing all his experiments alone.
(C) Before scientists found out about germs, people believed evil spirits made us sick or that it happened because we did bad things.
(D) Pasteur's method of getting doctors to wash their hands and sterilize tools and boiling liquids like milk and wine to kill germs are still used today.
(E) Governments today only allow doctors to sell liquids that have not been boiled because they can help sick people.

Check-up

A. Choose the correct answers.

1. What should you do when answering a sentence simplification question?
   (A) Eliminate answer choices that use some important details to summarize the main idea of the highlighted sentence.
   (B) Eliminate answer choices that contradict the message of the highlighted sentence.
   (C) Eliminate answer choices that use important details from the highlighted sentence to convey the same meaning in fewer words.
   (D) Eliminate answer choices that paraphrase the highlighted sentence.

2. When answering a sentence simplification question, you should
   (A) eliminate answer choices that use important details from the highlighted sentence to convey a different meaning.
   (B) eliminate answer choices that paraphrase the highlighted sentence.
   (C) eliminate answer choices that use some important details to summarize the main idea of the highlighted sentence.
   (D) eliminate answer choices that use important details from the highlighted sentence to convey the same meaning in fewer words.

Key Vocabulary Practice

B. Fill in the blanks with the correct words.

scientific	species	experiments	Bible	evil
origin	microscopes	ignore	philosopher	micro-organisms

1. The _____ story of Adam and Eve tells about the snake in the Garden of Eden.

2. It is dangerous to _____ pain and better to see a doctor if you get hurt.

3. Scientists often do _____ with mice and rats to check the effects of drugs.

4. Astronomers are still trying to figure out the exact _____ of the universe.

5. Cockroaches are a very interesting insect _____ and can survive nuclear bomb explosions.

6. Hitler was considered a very _____ man because he killed so many people.

7. The German _____ Karl Marx wrote the book *Das Kapital*.

8. Doctors use _____ to look at slides containing bacterial diseases.

9. The _____ causes of diseases were not known for hundreds of years.

10. It is amazing to think how many _____ fly unseen in the air around us.

[04] Human Biology

Getting Ready to Read

A. Learn the words.

Key Vocabulary

lack	having too little of something; a shortage
patient	a sick person who is cared for, usually by doctors or nurses in a hospital
medication	pills or other treatment that help the sick get well
addicted	cannot do without something; dependent on
melatonin	a chemical made by the body that plays a role in sleep

TOEFL® Vocabulary

integral	essential; of great importance; intrinsic
ultimately	finally; at the end of
fluctuation	changes; a repeated rise and fall
aid	something that helps or supports
supplement	additional help; something that supplies a deficiency

B. Learn the question types.

TOEFL® Question Types

Inference
Which of the following can be inferred about X?
The author of the passage implies that X
Which of the following can be inferred from paragraph X about Y?

- Incorrect answer choices may include an inference that is irrelevant to the passage.
- Incorrect answer choices may include an inference that is relevant but not supported by information in the passage.

Rhetorical Purpose
The author discusses X in paragraph Y in order to
Why does the author mention X?
The author uses X as an example of

- Incorrect answer choices may include a false or inaccurate purpose according to the information in the passage.
- Incorrect answer choices may include a purpose that is relevant to the passage but not to the words or actions asked about in the question.

C. Read the passage. Number each paragraph with the correct main idea or purpose.

1. Causes of sleeping problems
2. Importance of sleep
3. Medical help for sleeping problems
4. Healthy ways to sleep better
5. Sleeping problems

Sleep

___ All human beings need sleep to live. Getting enough sleep is as integral to our health as food or water. It is during the sleeping hours that our bodies rest and repair themselves. In fact, lack of sleep can ultimately do such harm people may die younger because of it. Studies have shown that people who get less sleep often die younger than those who get more.

___ Many people struggle to sleep well. They experience fluctuations in their sleeping patterns. They wake up in the middle of the night a lot. They feel tired and lack energy to do daily tasks.

___ Doctors and scientists have studied sleeping problems. They found that people who have a lot of stress at work or who do not exercise enough often have trouble sleeping.

___ Doctors sometimes give patients sleeping aids to help them sleep. This can include medication such as sleeping pills. This is not always a good idea because patients can get addicted to these pills.

___ Using vitamins or food supplements such as melatonin, eating well, and exercising are better for you. Drinking something warm before bedtime can also help you sleep but eating a heavy meal is not a good idea.

Note-taking

D. Complete the summary notes by filling in the blanks.

Topic: _____

Introduction: All _____ need _____ to live. Enough sleep is _____ to health. During the sleeping hours our bodies rest and _____.
_____ show that people who get less sleep often _____.

Sleeping problems: Many people _____ well.
They experience _____ in their sleeping _____.
_____ up in the _____ of the night a lot. Feel _____ and _____ energy.

Studies: Doctors and _____ have studied sleeping _____. Found that _____ with lots of _____ at work or who don't _____ enough have _____ sleeping.

Medication: Doctors sometimes give patients sleeping _____. Can include _____ such as _____.

Other solutions: Use vitamins or food _____. Eating _____ _____. Drinking something _____.
Don't eat a _____.

E. Choose the correct answers.

1. What does the author infer about getting too little sleep in paragraph 1?

(A) You may die at a younger age if you get too little sleep.

(B) You will die if you don't get enough sleep.

2. According to the passage, which of the following about sleep is NOT true?

(A) Our bodies rest and heal when we sleep.

(B) Sleep is not as important for health as water or food.

3. The word fluctuations in paragraph 2 is closest in meaning to

(A) changes

(B) problems

4. What can be inferred from the passage about sleeping pills?

(A) They can be dangerous because people get addicted to them.

(B) They are a very useful way of getting enough sleep.

TOEFL® Vocabulary Practice

F. Fill in the blanks with the correct words.

supplements	fluctuations	ultimately	aid	integral

1. There are often _____ in the oil price due to war in the Middle East.

2. Ascorbic acid and flax seed oil are excellent health _____.

3. The Allies _____ won World War II because of US support.

4. Europe and North America provide Africa with a lot of financial _____.

5. The concept of freedom is a(n) _____ part of the US constitution.

Practice

A. Learn the words.

Key Vocabulary

pregnant	with child; carrying an unborn child inside you
fertile	able to produce; able to have children
blood pressure	the force of blood against the walls of cells as pushed by the heart
sonar	sound system using echoes; found in nature as sounds made by bats and dolphins
heartbeat	the pulse of the heart as it pumps blood

TOEFL® Vocabulary

conceive	to become pregnant; to make a baby
mature	fully developed; older; adult
defect	a fault or problem; something wrong with something
utilize	to make use of; to use
induce	to cause or speed up something; to make it happen

Reading Passage

B. Read the passage and underline the key information.

Pregnancy

Women find it harder to get pregnant as they grow older. This is because they become less fertile. After the age of about thirty-eight it is often more difficult to conceive. A woman's body may not be as healthy as when she was younger.

Luckily, there are a lot of ways to help mature women have children these days, but they still have to be very careful. Babies born from older women are more likely to have birth defects. That is why doctors do so much to keep pregnant older women healthy.

They check the pregnant woman's blood pressure and weight. They tell her what to eat and what not to eat. They also do tests to see if the baby is healthy. They can look at the baby using a special machine. They do this by rubbing a special gel onto the woman's stomach. Then they look at the baby using a sonar machine. The machine uses the gel to see through skin into the body. Doctors can check the baby's heartbeat, how big it is, and many other things with sonar.

They often utilize technology to help women give birth to healthy babies. This is useful not only during pregnancy but also during birth. In the past, birth was a very dangerous thing. There were many things that could go wrong. These days, it is less dangerous. If women are in danger, doctors can even induce birth. They use medicine to do so.

C. Choose the correct answers.

1. What can be inferred from the passage about older women having babies?

(A) It is very dangerous to do so and your child will have birth defects.

(B) It is harder to do so but if you are careful you can have a healthy baby.

2. The word defects in paragraph 2 is closest in meaning to

(A) fault   (B) illness

3. According to the passage, doctors use sonar machines to

(A) check the baby's heartbeat, size, and other things

(B) check the mother's heartbeat and blood pressure

4. The word they in the last paragraph refers to

(A) doctors   (B) mothers

TOEFL® Vocabulary Practice

D. Fill in the blanks with the correct words.

| defect | induce | mature | utilized | conceive |

1. It is easier for women to _____ at certain times of the month than others.

2. If you buy an appliance with a(n) _____, you should return it to the store at once.

3. Girls are usually more _____ than boys during the teenage years.

4. When a woman's contractions are too slow, doctors often _____ birth.

5. Technology is _____ by more people today than twenty years ago.

Read the passage.

The Heart

The heart is an integral part of the human body. If our hearts do not work we will die. Hearts pump blood through our bodies, and every part of our bodies needs blood. This is because blood is full of oxygen which keeps us alive. A human heart has four parts, and each one is like a room. The top rooms take the blood in and the bottom rooms push the blood out. The right side of the heart takes in blood without oxygen. It pushes this blood to our lungs where it fills with oxygen. Then this blood is pushed to the left side of the heart. The left side pumps the oxygen-rich blood out into the rest of our body.

The human heart starts to beat twenty-one days after a woman conceives. The baby's heartbeat is faster than its pregnant mother's. A mature adult who is in good health has a heartbeat of about seventy-two beats per minute. At first, a baby has a heartbeat of about eighty beats per minute but later it gets even faster. Doctors use sonar machines to listen to the baby's heartbeat in its mother's stomach.

Healthy adult hearts weigh about 250 to 350 grams. If people do not live healthy lives, their hearts can develop defects and one of these defects is an enlarged heart which is very dangerous. Enlarged hearts can weigh as much as 1000 grams or one kilogram. Other people are just unlucky and they are born with heart defects. Their hearts do not have a steady beat. Instead, there are fluctuations in their heartbeat. These people need a special aid called a pacemaker and they have to utilize this machine their whole lives.

When we get older, our hearts become weaker and if our blood pressure is high, we can have a heart attack. This means our hearts will stop working. If someone has a heart attack, doctors can induce a heartbeat with another special machine called a defibrillator. They can also give people medication to help. Ultimately it is better to keep your heart healthy through a healthy lifestyle. Always get lots of exercise, eat lots of fruit and vegetables and don't eat too much red meat.

Choose the correct answers.

1. The word integral in paragraph 1 is closest in meaning to
   (A) very useful
   (B) very helpful
   (C) very interesting
   (D) very important

2. The highlighted it in paragraph 1 refers to
   (A) blood
   (B) heart
   (C) lungs
   (D) human body

3. According to paragraph 2, which of the following is true of a baby's heartbeat?

(A) Its heart beats at the same rate as its mother's heart.

(B) A baby's heart beats at about seventy-two beats per minute.

(C) A baby's heart only starts to beat twenty-one days after the baby has been conceived.

(D) A baby's heartbeat slows down after twenty-one days.

4. Why does the author mention heart defects?

(A) She wants to warn people that their hearts are in danger.

(B) She thinks heart defects are interesting for the reader.

(C) She wants readers to look after their health so their hearts don't get sick.

(D) She wants more people to get pacemaker machines.

5. What can be inferred about heart attacks from paragraph 4?

(A) Eating red meat helps one avoid heart attacks.

(B) People with high blood pressure are more likely to get heart attacks.

(C) Older people are more likely to get them because they eat too much red meat.

(D) Younger people are more likely to get them because they have weaker hearts.

6. Complete the table below by selecting the appropriate phrases from the answer choices and match them with the heading where they belong. TWO of the answer choices will not be used. **This question is worth 3 points**.

(A) Enlarged, weighs up to one kilogram

(B) Beats seventy-two times in one minute

(C) Needs medication to stop heart attack

(D) Beats about eighty times in one minute

(E) Weighs between 250 and 350 grams

(F) Heartbeat fluctuates and needs pacemaker

(G) Gets much faster over time

Healthy adult heart

- _____
- _____

Sick adult heart

- _____
- _____
- _____

Check-up

A. Choose the correct answers.

1. What should you do when answering an inference question?

(A) Eliminate answer choices that contain inferences that are relevant to the main idea of the passage.

(B) Eliminate answer choices that contain inferences that are not relevant to the main idea of the passage.

(C) Eliminate answer choices that contain inferences based on information not included in the passage.

(D) Eliminate answer choices that contain inferences that are supported by information in the passage.

2. When answering a rhetorical purpose question, you should

(A) select an answer choice that presents a purpose not related to the words or actions asked about in the question.

(B) eliminate answer choices that contain purposes supported by the information in the passage.

(C) select an answer choice that presents a purpose related to the passage but not the question asked.

(D) eliminate answer choices that contain purposes not supported by the information in the passage.

Key Vocabulary Practice

B. Fill in the blanks with the correct words.

sonar	pregnant	patients	heartbeats	blood pressure
fertile	addicted	melatonin	lack	medication

1. A(n) _____ of good education is a big problem for job seekers in South Africa.

2. Some people believe Princess Diana was _____ when she died in 1997.

3. When people become angry, their _____ often rises.

4. The poet, Samuel Taylor Coleridge, was _____ to the drug opium.

5. Your body starts to produce _____ when it gets dark to help you sleep.

6. When _____ leave hospital they usually have to exit in a wheelchair.

7. Dolphins and whales communicate with each other using _____.

8. In some cultures, women who are not _____ are rejected by their husbands.

9. Athletes have slower _____ than most people due to their fitness.

10. Type-C diabetics often have to inject themselves with insulin _____.

Getting Ready to Read

A. Learn the words.

Key Vocabulary

manager	the person responsible for overseeing the running of a business
appreciate	to be thankful; to acknowledge the importance of
relation	a connection or association between people
brief	short in time
productive	the quality of getting work done

TOEFL® Vocabulary

motivation	a reason to do something
enhance	to make better
compile	to gather and organize
cooperative	helpful; the quality of working together effectively
termination	firing; job loss

B. Learn the question types.

TOEFL® Question Types

Insert Text

Look at the four squares [■] that indicate where the following sentence could be added to the passage.

[You will see a sentence in bold.]

Where would the sentence best fit?

- Incorrect answer choices may not fit with the logical sequence of ideas in the passage.
- Incorrect answer choices may not contain the correct grammatical structure to fit in with sentences before or after the square.
- Incorrect answer choices may contain inappropriate transitional words or phrases.

C. Read the passage. Number each paragraph with the correct main idea or purpose.

1. How a manager can be a good leader
2. Why a manager should be a good leader
3. The importance of workers' perceptions of the purpose of the interview
4. Why regular interviews are a good idea

Effective Management and the Employee Interview

___ The manager's job is to make sure the business is running well. A big part of the business is the workers. They have to be doing their best for the business to be doing its best. So managers have to make sure workers are doing their best. To do this they have to be good leaders.

___ Good leaders should understand why some people work hard and some don't. ■ 1) Then they can provide motivation for workers. ■ 2) Money is not the only motivation for workers. ■ 3) Workers want to know that they are appreciated. They want to feel like they are part of the company's success. ■ 4)

___ Managers need to enhance worker-manager relations. One way is to do brief interviews every three months. This allows managers to compile information. Workers can express their attitudes toward certain policies. Then they feel like they are being listened to. This makes them likely to be more cooperative.

___ ■ 5) It is important that workers know the purpose of the interview. If they think it is an evaluation they will perform differently. ■ 6) The fear of termination can effect their level of honesty. ■ 7) They should see the interview as a chance to express themselves. ■ 8) Then it will be more productive.

D. Complete the summary notes by filling in the blanks.

Topic:	_____
Importance of leadership:	Managers have to make sure the business is _____. Have to make sure workers are _____. Need to be good _____.
How to lead:	Should understand what makes people _____. Must provide _____. Workers want to feel _____.
Interviews:	Interviews can improve _____. Chance to _____ information. Workers can _____ their attitudes and feel like they are _____. Workers are more likely to be _____.
Employee understanding:	Workers should know the _____. They shouldn't think it is an _____. If they see it as a chance to express themselves it will be _____.

E. Choose the correct answers.

1. Look at the four squares (■) that indicate where the following sentence could be added to the passage.

If they feel that way, they will work harder to make sure the company succeeds.

Where would the sentence best fit?

(A) Square 1
(B) Square 2
(C) Square 3
(D) Square 4

2. Look at the four squares (■) that indicate where the following sentence could be added to the passage.

If the workers and managers aren't working together in the interview, it will be a waste of time.

Where would the sentence best fit?

(A) Square 5
(B) Square 6
(C) Square 7
(D) Square 8

TOEFL® Vocabulary Practice

F. Fill in the blanks with the correct words.

motivation	enhance	compiled	cooperative	termination

1. People often add some salt to _____ the flavor of some soups.

2. She _____ some of the author's less known short stories into a book.

3. Harassment will not be tolerated among the staff and will result in _____.

4. The children became more _____ when they realized they had a common goal.

5. The possibility of promotion was her _____ for putting in the extra hours at work.

Practice

A. Learn the words.

supply	the quantity of goods or services that are available
demand	the quantity of goods or services that consumers care to purchase
x-axis	the horizontal line on a graph that measures quantity
y-axis	the vertical line on a graph that measures price
intersection	the point where two lines meet

TOEFL® Vocabulary

commodity	a thing of value
inclination	slope
coincide	to happen at the same time as
insight	a glimpse or understanding of the nature of a thing
aggregate	total

Reading Passage

B. Read the passage and underline the key information.

Supply and Demand

Why do commodities cost what they do? ■ 1) How is the price decided? The answer lies in the law of supply and demand. ■ 2) It states that as demand increases, price increases. Alternatively, as demand decreases, price decreases. ■ 3) Supply is also important. ■ 4) As supply increases, price decreases. As supply decreases, price increases.

This idea can be shown in a graph. The x-axis shows the amount. The y-axis shows the price. The demand is shown as a line with a downward sloping inclination. That means that as the amount of demand increases, the price increases. This makes sense. If a lot of people want something, they are willing to pay more for it.

■ 5) But you have to consider supply, too. ■ 6) It is shown as an upward sloping line. ■ 7) Here, an increase in supply coincides with a decrease in demand. This makes sense because if suppliers have too much of something, they want to get rid of it. Therefore, they try to sell it at a lower price. ■ 8)

So, the demand line and the supply line form an X. The intersection of that X will be the best price. This simple rule also gives us insight into what is happening in the economy. We can see what the aggregate demand is for all goods and services in the economy at a given price. We do this by adding together the individual demand curves for each sector. We can look at aggregate supply, too. This is the total supply in the economy during a specific period of time.

C. Choose the correct answers.

1. Look at the four squares (■) that indicate where the following sentence could be added to the passage.

This is a fundamental law in economics.

Where would the sentence best fit?

(A) Square 1   (B) Square 2
(C) Square 3   (D) Square 4

2. Which of the following can be inferred about consumers?

(A) They do not want goods that are in short supply.
(B) They compete with one another for scarce resources.

3. Why does the author mention the graph?

(A) Because it will help students learn how to determine prices of goods
(B) So students can visualize the relationship between supply and demand

4. Look at the four squares that indicate where the following sentence could be added to the passage.

That's why they have sales.

Where would the sentence best fit?

(A) Square 5   (B) Square 6
(C) Square 7   (D) Square 8

D. Fill in the blanks with the correct words.

commodities	inclination	coincides	insights	aggregate

1. Having grown up in a troubled home, the teacher had _____ into her student's problems.

2. He made his fortune by setting up a website where people can buy and sell _____.

3. My birthday _____ with the full moon this year.

4. We will add each department's expense account to come up with the _____ expenses.

5. We had to increase the _____ of the ramp or else it would have been too long.

Read the passage.

Market Economy

Competition is the most important thing in a market economy. Firms compete with one another for business. This helps to keep prices reasonable. To get some insight into how this works, think of what would happen if firms cooperated. The motivation of every firm is to enhance their profit margins. One way to do this is to increase price. If all of the firms were cooperating, they could set any price. The consumer would have to pay it or do without the commodity being sold.

In general, firms don't cooperate. They compete. Consider this example. A pencil costs twenty-five cents to make. Firm A makes pencils and sells them for two dollars. Firm B sells them for one dollar. Firm B's pencils are just as good as Firm A's. Which firm will make more money? Well, if they sold an equal number of pencils, Firm A would. But they won't sell an equal number of pencils. Firm B will sell more. This is because consumers will look for the best price. So, Firm B will sell more pencils and earn a greater profit. So, in general, the firm that offers the best product for the best price should turn the best profit. Increasing price will not enhance profit margins unless the competition does the same.

There are situations in a market economy where no competition exists. This is called a monopoly. When a firm has no competition, it has a monopoly. ■ 1) It can virtually set any price because consumers have only one option. ■ 2) The other option is to do without the commodity. So the firm needs to compile data on the maximum amount consumers are willing to pay for their product. Then they can charge that price. Generally, though, if a firm has a monopoly, it won't last. ■ 3) The opening of new firms to compete with them will coincide with their initial success. ■ 4) A steep inclination in the demand curve for a certain product will signal other suppliers to provide it. Furthermore, there are laws in place that keep firms from maintaining a monopoly in any industry.

Choose the correct answers.

1. Why does the author mention pencils?

(A) To demonstrate the principle of competition
(B) As an example of an industry with a monopoly
(C) To demonstrate how production costs effect price
(D) As an example of an exception to a general rule

2. The word same in the passage refers to

(A) enhancing profit margins

(B) increasing price

(C) offer the best product

(D) offer the best price

3. Look at the four squares (■) that indicate where the following sentence could be added to the passage.

It is the optimal scenario for a business.

Where would the sentence best fit?

(A) Square 1

(B) Square 2

(C) Square 3

(D) Square 4

4. The word charge in the passage is closest in meaning to

(A) attack

(B) accuse

(C) credit

(D) demand

5. All of the following were mentioned as factors determining price EXCEPT

(A) price offered by competing firms

(B) price consumers are willing to pay

(C) number of firms competing

(D) cost of producing products

6. An introductory sentence for a brief summary of the passage is provided below. Complete the summary by selecting the THREE answer choices that express the most important ideas in the passage. Some sentences do not belong in the summary because they express ideas that are not presented in the passage or are minor ideas in the passage. **This question is worth 2 points.**

Competition keeps firms from charging too much.

(A) If firms cooperated in setting prices, prices would be too high.

(B) Competition keeps prices low because consumers seek the best price.

(C) Pencil makers earn huge profits because pencils are so cheap to make.

(D) A firm has a monopoly if it has no competition, but this is rare.

(E) It's against the law to compete with a monopoly.

Check-up

A. Choose the correct answers.

When answering an insert text question, you should

(A) eliminate answer choices that present ideas that form a logical progression to the ideas presented before the square.

(B) eliminate answer choices whose grammatical structure fits in with the sentences before and after the square.

(C) eliminate answer choices that present ideas that do not fit with the logical flow of the sentences around the square.

(D) eliminate answer choices that contain appropriate transitional words or phrases.

Key Vocabulary Practice

B. Fill in the blanks with the correct words.

manager	appreciate	relations	brief	productive
supply	demand	x-axis	y-axis	intersection

1. As you move right along the _____, quantity gets bigger.

2. Some people are more _____ in the morning because they have more time to themselves.

3. The teacher's comments were _____ and emphasized the student's strong points.

4. As you move up the _____, price gets higher.

5. A(n) _____ of a company usually has the most responsibilities.

6. Most women _____ flowers on special occasions.

7. There was a huge _____ for the new video game this Christmas.

8. The recent scandal has put a strain on inter-staff _____.

9. No one knew the doll would be so popular. _____ couldn't keep up with demand.

10. The _____ of the supply curve and the demand curve determines the optimal price.

[06] Cultural Studies

Getting Ready to Read

A. Learn the words.

Key Vocabulary

anthropology	the scientific study of people and cultures
explorer	someone who searches and travels to discover new places and things
Aborigine	the first people to live in Australia; a primitive, tribal people
hut	a small, rough-built house or shelter
way of life	how people live, what they do, their culture, beliefs and practices

TOEFL® Vocabulary

definition	an explanation of the exact meaning of a word
undertake	to commit to doing something
indigenous	native born; coming from that place; the first to live or be there
uncivilized	not having developed or progressed; rough, savage, without refinement
conduct	the way we behave or act

B. Learn the question types.

TOEFL® Question Types

Summary

An introductory sentence for a brief summary of the passage is provided below.
Complete the summary by selecting the THREE answer choices that express the most
important ideas in the passage. Some sentences do not belong in the summary because
they express ideas that are not presented in the passage or are minor ideas in the passage.
This question is worth 2 points.

A correct summary sentence will be written in bold followed by three spaces for correct answers.

- Incorrect answer choices may contain minor details from the passage.
- Incorrect answer choices may include details not mentioned in the passage.
- One point is awarded for getting two of three correct, so fill in all spaces even if you are not certain.

C. Read the passage. Number each paragraph with the correct main idea and purpose.

1. Information about Péron's thoughts on Aborigine culture
2. Information about Aborigine culture
3. Information on Péron's hopes for studying other cultures
4. An explanation of what anthropology is
5. Information about Francois Péron's travels

Francois Péron

___ It is difficult to find a good definition for the word "anthropology." It is easiest to say it is the study of human cultures.

___ The word was first used by a French explorer called Francois Péron. In 1801, he undertook a journey to Australia with some scientists. He wanted to learn more about the indigenous people who lived there. Later, he visited the island of Tasmania which is part of Australia. In both places, he met people called Aborigines.

___ They were a big tribe who lived a very simple life. They hunted animals for meat, fished in the sea, and grew vegetables. They lived in huts, wore few clothes, and spoke a strange language. They liked to sit around a big fire and tell stories. They also loved to make music and art.

___ Péron studied their way of life carefully. He wrote down everything about them. He knew most Europeans would think Aborigines were uncivilized. He did not think so. He thought their conduct was interesting. Their culture was simple but it was not bad.

___ Péron wanted people in Europe to see that the world is full of people with different ways of life. So, he made up this new word for studying cultures.

D. Complete the summary notes by filling in the blanks.

Topic: _____

Introduction: _____ is the study of _____.

Francois Péron: French _____, first to use this word. _____ a trip to _____ with scientists in _____. Wanted to learn about _____. Also visited island of _____. Met _____.

Aborigines: Big _____ who lived a _____ life. Hunted _____, fished, and grew _____. Lived in _____, wore few _____, spoke a strange _____. Liked to tell _____ round big _____, make _____ and art.

Péron's studies: Studied Aborigine's _____ and _____ down everything. Knew most _____ would think they were _____. He thought _____ was interesting and culture _____.

Péron's wish: Wanted Europeans to see that the _____ is full of people with _____ cultures, so made up _____.

E. Choose the correct answers.

1. Summary

An introductory sentence for a brief summary of the passage is provided below. Complete the summary by selecting the THREE answer choices that express the most important ideas in the passage. Some sentences do not belong in the summary because they express ideas that are not presented in the passage or are minor ideas in the passage.

Anthropology is the study of human cultures.

(A) Péron met the Aborigines who had a very simple way of life which he studied carefully.

(B) Péron knew that most Europeans would think Aborigines were uncivilized because they wore few clothes.

(C) The word was first used by explorer Francois Péron, who traveled to Australia and Tasmania in 1801 to study indigenous tribes.

(D) Aborigines lived in huts, spoke English, and loved music and art.

(E) He found the Aborigines interesting and wanted Europeans to see that cultures should be studied.

2. The word explorer in paragraph 2 is closest in meaning to

(A) traveler   (B) scientist

3. According to paragraph 3, which of the following is true of Aborigines?

(A) They spoke English very well.

(B) They had a great love of music.

4. Which of the following can be inferred from the passage about Francois Péron?

(A) He thought differently about culture than most Europeans of his time.

(B) He liked Aborigines more than Europeans because they were uncivilized.

F. Fill in the blanks with the correct words.

conduct   indigenous   undertook   definition   uncivilized

1. The _____ people of Mexico were called Mayans.

2. President Richard Nixon resigned in 1974 because of bad and illegal _____.

3. The character, Tarzan, was raised by monkeys and was therefore very _____.

4. In 1953, Sir Edmund Hilary _____ the ascent of Mount Everest in Nepal.

5. The _____ of the word "aloof" is to be shy and to avoid other people.

Practice

A. Learn the words.

Key Vocabulary

marry	to take a husband or wife
wedding	the ceremony and celebration when two people marry
raise	to bring up and look after
suffragette	name for women who fought for voting rights (suffrage) in late nineteenth century
marches	to walk with others, usually to protest something

TOEFL® Vocabulary

contemporary	current; to do with today; this time period
rank	a position of power you hold, usually in the military or in government
persistent	to keep fighting or asking for something until you get it
feminist	a person, usually female, who believes men and women must have equal rights
gender	your sex; male or female

Reading Passage

B. Read the passage and underline the key information.

The Feminist Movement

In many societies, women have less power than men. When they are young they have to listen to their fathers. They may not choose who they want to marry. Their husband is chosen by their family. This often makes women sad because they do not love these men. After the wedding, they have to do what their husband tells them to do. In these societies, women are usually not allowed to work. They have to stay at home and raise children because this is tradition.

In many contemporary cultures, these rules and traditions have changed. Women have much more freedom now. They are allowed to have jobs and they can hold powerful ranks. They can even become president. These changes have happened very slowly over hundreds of years.

It is because of the persistent work of women who fought for more freedom. They were called feminists. They wanted more rights and they wanted to be able to do all the same things men did. They did not think a person's gender should decide what they could or could not do. They believed that if you could do something well, it did not matter if you were a man or a women.

The first feminists came from England. They were called suffragettes. They fought to get the vote. It took many years and many marches. In 1918, the government passed a law that said women who were over the age of thirty and who owned land could vote.

C. Choose the correct answers.

1. An introductory sentence for a brief summary of the passage is provided below. Complete the summary by selecting the THREE answer choices that express the most important ideas in the passage. Some sentences do not belong in the summary because they express ideas that are not presented in the passage or are minor ideas in the passage.

The role of women is different in different societies.

(A) Marrying the man chosen by their family makes many women in traditional societies sad.

(B) The first feminists were the suffragettes who fought for the vote in England in 1918.

(C) In many traditional societies, women do not have power and must obey their husbands and fathers, stay home, and raise children.

(D) Feminists believe that a woman can become president.

(E) In many contemporary societies, women can work and hold high ranks because of the work of feminists who fought for equal rights for women.

2. The word contemporary is closest in meaning to

(A) conservative (B) modern

3. According to the passage, which of the following is NOT true of feminists?

(A) They believe women are stronger and smarter than men.

(B) They did not think gender should decide what a person can do.

4. The author uses suffragettes as an example of

(A) feminists who changed the roles and rights of women

(B) women who wanted to become leaders in England

D. Fill in the blanks with the correct words.

gender	contemporary	feminist	persistent	rank

1. Modern and _____ art is very different from the art of the Renaissance.

2. Doctors can tell the _____ of a baby while still inside its mother's stomach.

3. To succeed in business, you need to be very _____ and ambitious.

4. The lowest _____ you can be in the army is a Private.

5. Germaine Greer is a _____ writer from Australia who wrote *The Female Eunuch*.

Read the passage.

Apache Indians

Apache Indians are indigenous people from North America. There are many North American Indian tribes like the Apaches. None of them are from India. They were called Indians by mistake. In 1492, the Spanish explorer, Christopher Columbus, undertook a voyage to find a quick sea route to India from Spain. He traveled in a ship and got lost. He came to a place that he thought was India. He called the people he met there "Indians." But he was really in North America.

When Europeans first met the Apaches they thought they were uncivilized. They believed the Apaches did not have a good culture. They thought their conduct was bad. This was because the Apaches went to war against them. The Apaches did not want Europeans to take their land. That is why they fought them. The Europeans were very persistent. In the end, they beat the Apaches and took their land. The Apaches were no longer free. They had to obey the laws of the United States.

The contemporary view of Apaches is very different. ■ 1) Thanks to anthropology, we now know a lot about them. ■ 2) They learned that the Apaches were one of the largest and most well-known North American Indian tribes. ■ 3) They lived around Texas and Arizona. They had a very interesting culture. ■ 4) They were a very proud and strong nation.

Unlike Aborigines and other indigenous peoples, Apaches did not live in huts. This was because they moved around a lot. They lived in tents made of leather and sticks. The tents were easy to move and light to carry. They were built by the Apache women. Apaches did jobs by following their gender roles. Men hunted and went to war against their enemies. Their leader was called a chief. This was the highest rank in the Apache tribe. Women built tents, raised children, and cooked food.

These women were not feminists. They were happy to marry who their fathers told them to. Their weddings were held with lots of music, dancing, and eating. One thing that was unusual was that the husband joined his wife's family. He left his own family to live with them. In most traditional cultures, the woman usually joins her husband's family.

Choose the correct answers.

1. The word indigenous in paragraph 1 is closest in meaning to

   (A) native   (B) foreign

   (C) dangerous   (D) tribal

2. The highlighted word they in paragraph 2 refers to

   (A) Europeans   (B) Apaches

   (C) Spanish explorers   (D) North Americans

3. According to the passage, the Apaches fought the Europeans because

   (A) they were uncivilized and hated Europeans
   (B) they wanted to make Europeans obey their laws
   (C) their culture was to go to war against other people
   (D) they wanted to protect their land from being taken

4. Look at the four squares (■) that indicate where the following sentence could be added to the passage.

Scientists studied their culture and discovered many things about them.

Where would the sentence best fit?

   (A) Square 1   (B) Square 2
   (C) Square 3   (D) Square 4

5. Why does the author mention Aborigines in paragraph 4?

   (A) To show how Aborigines and Apaches are the same
   (B) To show how Apache homes are different from those of other indigenous people
   (C) To compare the way of life of Aborigines and other indigenous people
   (D) To show that Aborigines were smarter and more developed than Apaches

6. An introductory sentence for a brief summary of the passage is provided below. Complete the summary by selecting the THREE answer choices that express the most important ideas in the passage. Some sentences do not belong in the summary because they express ideas that are not presented in the passage or are minor ideas in the passage.

Apache Indians are native people from North America and have a very interesting culture.

   (A) The Apaches were a proud nation who divided roles by gender so that women cooked and raised children and men hunted and went to war against their enemies.
   (B) Columbus wanted to travel to Spain, got lost and ended up in North America.
   (C) Long ago, Europeans believed that Apaches were uncivilized but studies have shown they were not.
   (D) The tents they lived in were very light to carry and made of leather and sticks.
   (E) Apache women were not feminists—they married the men their fathers chose, and their weddings were held with lots of dancing and eating.

Check-up

A. Choose the correct answers.

1. What should you do when answering a summary question?

   (A) Leave one answer space empty if you are not certain of a correct answer.
   (B) Eliminate sentences that include important details from the passage.
   (C) Leave all the answer spaces blank if you are not certain of the correct answers.
   (D) Eliminate sentences that include minor details from the passage.

Key Vocabulary Practice

B. Fill in the blanks with the correct words.

explorer	huts	raised	marches	anthropology
way of life	suffragette	wedding	Aborigines	married

1. Harvard University has an excellent _____ department.

2. The Berber people of Morocco have a nomadic _____.

3. Film actress Grace Kelly _____ Prince Rainier III of Monaco in 1956.

4. Americans held many protest _____ to try and end the Vietnam War.

5. Emmeline Pankhurst was a founder of the British _____ movement.

6. At a traditional Jewish _____, the couple break a glass during the ceremony.

7. Captain James Cook was a famous _____ and the Cook Islands are named after him.

8. Legend has it that Romulus and Remus were _____ by a she-wolf.

9. The Kikuyu people lived in _____ on the foothills of Mount Kenya.

10. The _____ of Australia play a musical instrument called a didgeridoo.

[Review 1]

Read the passage.

African Wood Sculpture

The indigenous people of Africa are famous for their wood sculptures. Many artists have an inclination to work with wood. This is because wood is easy to find in Africa. There are big forests in many African countries. Wood is also softer than stone or metal. This makes it easier to carve.

African sculptors have a great diversity of styles. Every country's sculptures are also different. Artists use many different kinds of wood. They make sculptures of many different sizes. Sometimes they make enormous sculptures. These sculptures can be two or three meters high. They also make small sculptures. These are only a few inches tall. Most of them look like animals or people. Sculptures of African animals like leopards, lions, and elephants are very common.

Africans also cut masks out of wood. When African people wear masks, they invoke spirits. They dance around and sing. They believe that the masks turn them into animals. They believe this will give them power if they fight in a war. They also believe the masks can turn them into people who have died. They do this so that people can speak to their family members who have died. It is forbidden to take off someone's mask when they have invoked a spirit. Long ago, people were killed for doing this.

The great Spanish artist, Pablo Picasso, was very interested in African wood sculpture. Many Europeans thought this art was uncivilized. Picasso did not. He had the insight to see how beautiful it was. Picasso was a very rigorous artist. He always worked very hard. He did not like to conform. He did not like to follow fashions. He always tried new things.

In 1907, he started to copy African styles. He studied the wooden sculptures of Africa. He studied the wooden masks. Then he painted a famous picture called, "The young ladies of Avignon." ■ 1) It showed girls who looked like they were wearing wood masks. ■ 2) People in Europe were shocked. ■ 3) The painting was very controversial. ■ 4) It was so different from other European art. People thought it was ugly. This painting made Picasso famous.

Choose the correct answers.

1. The word inclination in paragraph 1 is closest in meaning to
   (A) habit
   (B) obsession
   (C) duty
   (D) preference

2. All of the following are true of African sculptors EXCEPT

(A) they use many different kinds of wood
(B) they use wood because it is softer than stone or metal
(C) all their sculptures are enormous, up to two or three meters high
(D) most of their sculptures look like people or animals such as lions or elephants

3. The highlighted word they in paragraph 3 refers to

(A) African artists
(B) African people
(C) African spirits
(D) African warriors

4. Look at the four squares (■) that indicate where the following sentence could be added to the passage.

They were also all naked in the picture.

Where would the sentence best fit?

(A) Square 1
(B) Square 2
(C) Square 3
(D) Square 4

5. The author discusses Picasso in the last paragraph in order to

(A) show that European artists are not uncivilized like African artists
(B) discuss how controversial African art has been throughout history
(C) show how African art inspired one of the world's greatest artists
(D) indicate how easily Europeans are shocked by things that are different

6. An introductory sentence for a brief summary of the passage is provided below. Complete the summary by selecting the THREE answer choices that express the most important ideas in the passage. Some sentences do not belong in the summary because they express ideas that are not presented in the passage or are minor ideas in the passage. **This question is worth 2 points.**

Indigenous African wood sculpture is world famous.

(A) They carve animal and human figures and masks which are used in ceremonies, like war dances and calling the dead.
(B) All African sculptures are of animals that they are afraid of and in their war dances they believe they become these animals by wearing wood masks.
(C) Pablo Picasso was interested in African wood sculpture and copied these styles when he made his famous painting, "The young ladies of Avignon."
(D) African artists work in a diversity of styles, using wood because it is easy to find and soft, to create animal or human figures of many different sizes.
(E) Picasso's painting style changed a lot through his life and he was always trying new things.

Read the passage.

The Liver

When doctors study human biology, they learn about all our body parts. One of the most important body parts is the liver. Throughout human evolution, the liver has helped us become stronger. The liver is integral to our health because it helps break down food into good and bad bits. It breaks down fat and it stores sugar. It cleans our bodies of poisons. After a woman has conceived, the liver makes blood to keep the baby alive. The liver is a very large organ. This is because it has so much to do. It lies under our rib cage and is adjacent to our stomachs.

The older we get, the more likely we are to get a liver disease. That is why it is good to take supplements to stay healthy. Mature people face the risk of getting liver cancer. People who drink too much alcohol also risk getting liver diseases. This is because alcohol is like a poison. If you drink too much beer or wine or whiskey, you can make your liver very sick. Some people have very bad drinking problems. They should be prohibited from drinking. Ultimately, you can die from drinking too much.

Some people are lucky. If their liver is sick or has a defect, they can ask a doctor to cut it out. The doctor can find them a new, healthy liver. The sick person can undergo surgery. The doctor must cut their body open very carefully. Then he must expose the sick liver and take it out. Then he inserts the new liver. He carefully attaches it to the body. Doctors need a lot of perseverance to work like this. They have to be very accurate. If they are not, the liver will not attach. It takes many hours to put in a new liver.

When the doctor is finished, he will confine the person who has a new liver to a special room. ■ 1) Nurses have to look after the person very carefully for a few days. ■ 2) This is because the new liver is sometimes incompatible with that person's body. ■ 3) Sometimes the body cannot work with a new, strange liver inside it. ■ 4)

Choose the correct answers.

1. The word adjacent in paragraph 1 is closest in meaning to
   (A) beside
   (B) far
   (C) under
   (D) above

2. According to the passage, people who drink too much alcohol get liver diseases because
   (A) their livers are weaker than healthy people's livers
   (B) alcohol causes cancer
   (C) alcohol is a kind of poison
   (D) they are not prohibited from drinking

3. Which of the following can be inferred about the writer's attitude to drinking too much?

(A) She does not think it is a serious problem.
(B) She thinks it is dangerous and possibly life threatening.
(C) She is afraid of people who drink too much.
(D) She thinks too many people have problems because of alcohol.

4. Look at the four squares (■) that indicate where the following sentence could be added to the passage.

They have to watch them twenty-four hours a day.

Where would the sentence best fit?

(A) Square 1
(C) Square 3

(B) Square 2
(D) Square 4

5. Why does the writer mention how a doctor puts a new liver into the body?

(A) She admires doctors and wants to show the reader how clever they are.
(B) She wants readers to know about what can happen if you drink too much.
(C) She thinks that liver surgery is dangerous and people need to know that.
(D) She wants to show that liver surgery is a long, difficult process that takes time and care.

6. An introductory sentence for a brief summary of the passage is provided below. Complete the summary by selecting the THREE answer choices that express the most important ideas in the passage. Some sentences do not belong in the summary because they express ideas that are not presented in the passage or are minor ideas in the passage. **This question is worth 2 points.**

The liver is one of the human body's most important organs.

(A) The liver has not changed much during human evolution and was always very large.
(B) Older people and those who drink too much alcohol can get liver diseases like cancer, so it is important to look after your liver.
(C) Doctors do careful liver transplants for lucky patients who must be watched to see that their new livers are not incompatible.
(D) The liver is very large because it breaks down food and removes poisons from our body.
(E) Doctors who are not accurate and who do not have perseverance should not do liver transplants.

Read the passage.

The World Bank

The World Bank was founded in 1945. This coincided with the end of the second Word War. The years preceding 1945 had been terrible. Many countries that had opposed Germany had been bombed. Cities were destroyed. Many people had been displaced because of the war. The economic scenario looked bad for most of Europe. The leaders of countries like the US and Britain had a lot of integrity. They wanted to help re-build Europe. They undertook a project to create a bank that could enhance poor people's lives.

The bank's first loan was $250 million to France. The French had to utilize this money to re-build their country. They had to build new homes and apartments. They had to build new schools and hospitals. There was a lot to do. They did it quickly. They had a lot of motivation. They wanted their country to be beautiful again. By the 1960s, most of Western Europe was back to the way it had been before the war.

The World Bank's members were co-operative. They tried to work well together at all times. Rich countries gave money to the bank to help poor countries. People at the bank conducted studies to see who needed help. They compiled lists of countries that needed aid. They compiled information about what kind of help each country needed.

After Europe was re-built, the World Bank decided to help other poor countries in the rest of the world. Most of these countries were now outside of Europe. There were many countries that needed aid. Countries in Africa, Asia, and South America felt exploited by Europe for hundreds of years. ■ 1) They felt that Europe had grown rich by taking commodities from them. ■ 2) The Europeans had taken gold, silver, and other metals. ■ 3) They took wood and coal. They even took slaves. ■ 4)

The World Bank has spent the last forty-five years trying to help these poorer countries in many different ways. It loans money to these countries. The money is utilized to start businesses in poor countries and to create jobs. It is used for education and to buy medicine. It is used to fight diseases like HIV/Aids.

Choose the correct answers.

1. The word preceding in paragraph 1 is closest in meaning to

(A) between

(B) after

(C) before

(D) during

2. Which of the following best expresses the essential information in the highlighted sentence? Incorrect answers change the meaning in important ways or leave out essential information.

The economic scenario looked bad for most of Europe.

    (A) Europe had money problems that seemed as if they would be hard to solve.
    (B) The future development of Europe's industries and business were doomed.
    (C) The scene in Europe was bleak when it came to studying economics.
    (D) The money plan for Europe was not a good one and would make people poorer.

3. According to the passage, which of the following is NOT true of the World Bank?

    (A) It was started in 1945 after the war.
    (B) It made its first bank loan to France.
    (C) The bank loans money to poor countries to build schools and hospitals.
    (D) The bank only helps poor countries in Europe.

4. What can be inferred from the passage about poor countries in Africa, Asia, and South America?

    (A) They often blamed Europe that they were poor.
    (B) They hated Europeans because they were rich.
    (C) They wanted their gold and silver back.
    (D) The people were really poor because they were lazy.

5. Look at the four squares (■) that indicate where the following sentence could be added to the passage.

The Europeans used all these things to make their own countries richer.

Where would the sentence best fit?

    (A) Square 1   (B) Square 2
    (C) Square 3   (D) Square 4

6. Complete the table below by selecting the appropriate phrases from the answer choices and matching them to the correct heading. TWO of the answer choices will not be used. **This question is worth 2 points.**

    (A) Loaned $250 million to France

The World Bank 1945–1960

    (B) Loans funds to fight diseases like HIV
    (C) Run by African, Asian, and South American countries

- _____
- _____
- _____

    (D) Founding coincided with war end
    (E) Decided to help countries outside Europe

The World Bank after 1960

    (F) Helped re-build post war Europe
    (G) Decided to only help countries inside Europe

- _____
- _____

[07] Literature

Getting Ready to Read

A. Learn the words.

storyline	the main plot of a book, film or television show
run free	to have freedom or liberty to think or do as one likes
capture	to catch and keep, usually as a prisoner
imagination	creative power to form ideas and images in the mind
real	actually existing; not false

TOEFL® Vocabulary

pursue	to chase, hunt or follow
concept	an idea; something thought of
brainstorm	to think about something a lot and get many good ideas
chapter	a main division or part of something, usually of a book
pace	the speed at which something moves

B. Learn the question types.

TOEFL® Question Types

Vocabulary
The word X in the passage is closest in meaning to
In stating X, the author means that

- Incorrect answer choices may contain synonyms to words found near the word in question.
- Incorrect answer choices may contain correct meanings of the word if it were used in a different context.

Reference
The word X in the passage refers to
The phrase X in paragraph Y refers to

- Incorrect answer choices might include nouns and phrases found in the passage but are not referred to by the referent in question.
- Incorrect answer choices will not make sense when substituted in for the referent in question.

C. Read the passage. Number each paragraph with the correct main idea or purpose.

1. Information on novel structure and plot
2. Details on how to structure a story
3. Information on how to get ideas for a novel
4. Details on how to form characters
5. Information on what to give your readers

Writing Novels

___ Pursuing a writing career is not always easy and writing novels can be a long process. First, writers need to think of a good concept. They also have to think of a storyline. It helps to brainstorm when you are trying to think of a topic for your book. You should let your mind run free and write down every idea you get.

___ You will also need to divide your novel into chapters. Doing so helps to give structure to your book. You also need to develop your plot. It is very important that your story has a good pace because you will need to excite your reader.

___ You should try to capture their imagination from the very first page. They should want to read further. There should always be something to keep them reading. If there is no action, readers may get bored.

___ Don't have too many different storylines in your novel because this may confuse your reader. It is better to start with a simple story. You can develop it from there. Remember, it is easier to add to a story than to take away!

___ You should also develop your characters well. You should describe the way they look and think. They should seem like real people.

D. Complete the summary notes by filling in the blanks.

Topic:	_____
As career:	_____ one is not always easy. Writing novels can be _____. Think of a good _____ and _____. Let your mind _____ and write down _____.
Novel structure:	Divide into _____ to give _____. Develop your _____. Should have a good pace to _____.
Readers:	Try to _____ from very first page. Without _____, readers may get _____.
Storyline:	Don't have _____ as it may _____ your reader. Better to start with a _____ story and then _____ it. Easier to add to a story than to _____!
Characters:	Develop your _____ well and describe _____. Should _____ like _____ people.

E. Choose the correct answers.

1. The word concept in paragraph 1 is closest in meaning to

(A) an idea   (B) a story

2. The word pace in paragraph 2 is closest in meaning to

(A) rhythm   (B) speed

3. The phrase doing so in paragraph 2 refers to

(A) writing a first chapter
(B) dividing your book into chapters

4. The highlighted word it in paragraph 4 refers to

(A) your storyline   (B) your book

TOEFL® Vocabulary Practice

F. Fill in the blanks with the correct words.

brainstorm	pace	chapters	concepts	pursued

1. The police _____ Colombian drug lord, Pablo Escobar, for many years.

2. When faced with a serious problem, it helps to _____ solutions.

3. Olympic athlete Cathy Freeman can run 400 meters at a very fast _____.

4. The book, *Harry Potter and the Order of the Phoenix*, has thirty-eight _____.

5. Einstein's theories are full of _____ most people find hard to understand.

Practice

A. Learn the words.

prize	something that is won
award	something given for an achievement
newspaper	a paper printed daily or weekly giving people information on current events
fiction	a story that is not true but made up
press	the print news industry; those who work for newspapers or magazines

TOEFL® Vocabulary

journalist	someone who writes for newspapers or magazines; a reporter
drama	a play written for stage; something full of action and passion
allocation	a share of something (often money), put aside for a specific or special use
media	channels through which information is communicated to the public such as radio, television, newspapers, etc.
prospect	the idea of something being possible; a possibility

Reading Passage

B. Read the passage and underline the key information.

The Pulitzer Prize

The Pulitzer Prize is a special award for American journalists and writers. It is named after a man called Joseph Pulitzer.

He was born in Hungary in 1847. He moved to the US in 1864. He worked as a journalist for many years. He became very rich. Pulitzer loved America very much and he loved working for newspapers. He made a lot of money. When he died in 1911, he left most of it to Columbia University. Some of the money was to start a school for journalists. The rest of the money was for his prize.

Pulitzer really wanted to make sure that Americans kept writing wonderful books. He also wanted American newspapers to be the best in the world. He hoped that his prize would make writers and journalists want to do their best. He thought that if they could win money they would work harder.

Pulitzer was right. Writers did try harder because of his prize. They were happy to have an award that recognized them. The first prizes were given out in 1917. Today, there are twenty-one different prize allocations in total. Writers of fiction, poetry, and drama can win prizes. So can writers of American history. There is also one music prize. Press writers and photographers can win many different awards.

The American media has a lot of respect for writers who win. The prospect of winning always excites writers. It also makes them proud of their country.

C. **Choose the correct answers.**

1. The word journalist in paragraph 1 is closest in meaning to

   (A) reporter   (B) writer

2. The highlighted word they in paragraph 3 refers to

   (A) American newspapers   (B) American writers and journalists

3. According to the passage, which of the following is NOT true of Joseph Pulitzer?

   (A) He was born in Hungary and moved to America.
   (B) He was born in America and moved to Hungary.
   (C) He loved America and working as a journalist.

4. According to the passage, the first Pulitzers were awarded in

   (A) 1971
   (B) 1917

TOEFL® Vocabulary Practice

D. **Fill in the blanks with the correct words.**

drama	allocations	prospect	media	journalists

1. The _____ of getting into a good college makes scholars aim for high SAT scores.

2. The United Nations makes many fund _____ for humanitarian causes.

3. *Oedipus Rex* is the most famous _____ by the Greek playwright Sophocles.

4. In today's world we get our news from the mass _____.

5. Many _____ have been killed in Iraq since war started there in 2003.

Test

Read the passage.

Tom Wolfe

Tom Wolfe is one of America's most well-known writers. He was born in Richmond, Virginia in 1931. After university, he pursued a career as a journalist. The prospect of making money as a writer excited Wolfe. He was a very active member of the press and worked for many different newspapers. His first job was with *The Washington Post* where he worked for three years from 1959 to 1961. He won two journalism awards for his writing. One was for a news story he wrote about Cuba. The other prize was for a funny story he wrote. He moved to New York in 1962 to work at the *New York Herald Tribune*.

Wolfe became famous for being one of the writers to start a movement called New Journalism. This was a very interesting concept. These "New" journalists used their imagination to add things to newspaper stories that were not real. Their storylines mixed truth and fiction. They would write about a real event and then they would brainstorm ways of making it sound more interesting. They thought this gave their stories more action and better flow. Not everyone in the media liked this because they thought journalists should only write the truth.

Wolfe also wrote stories for magazines. His stories were collected and published. His most famous non-fiction book was *The Electric Kool-Aid Acid Test*. It came out in 1968. His book, *The Right Stuff*, about American astronauts was published in 1979.

Wolfe wrote his first novel in 1987. It was called *The Bonfire of the Vanities*. It was a story full of drama. It was about a rich white man whose girlfriend kills a poor black man in a car accident. ■ 1) This happens in the first few chapters of the book. ■ 2) The rich white man tries to save his girlfriend from being caught by police. ■ 3) He uses his money to do so. He also tells lies to protect her. ■ 4) He thinks the poor black man's life is not important. Many people wanted to read the book and it sold many copies. It was also made into a film and Wolfe was paid five million dollars by the film makers.

Choose the correct answers.

1. The word pursued in paragraph 1 is closest in meaning to
   (A) studied
   (B) considered
   (C) followed
   (D) investigated

2. The highlighted word they in paragraph 3 refers to
   (A) Tom Wolfe and his friends
   (B) the New Journalists
   (C) the Media
   (D) American writers

3. According to the passage, Tom Wolfe started New Journalism because

(A) he thought that writing only the truth in news stories was boring

(B) he wanted to be remembered for an interesting writing concept

(C) he believed news stories had more action and were more interesting this way

(D) he wanted to write novels and this was a good start because he used his imagination

4. What can be inferred about the plot of *The Bonfire of the Vanities?*

(A) It focuses on dishonest women who always get men to help them.

(B) It ends with a big fire in the city.

(C) It focuses on differences between rich and poor as well as black and white people.

(D) It focuses on the dangers of driving too fast.

5. Look at the four squares (■) that indicate where the following sentence could be added to the passage.

She is very scared of going to prison.

Where would the sentence best fit?

(A) Square 1

(B) Square 2

(C) Square 3

(D) Square 4

6. Summary

An introductory sentence for a brief summary of the passage is provided below. Complete the summary by selecting the THREE answer choices that express the most important ideas in the passage. Some sentences do not belong in the summary because they express ideas that are not presented in the passage or are minor ideas in the passage.

A writer and journalist Tom Wolfe has had an interesting career.

(A) He became famous for coming up with the writing concept New Journalism, which were news stories that had fictional elements.

(B) Wolfe was excited about making money and that is why he chose to become a writer.

(C) After publishing some non-fiction works he became a novelist and his first book, *The Bonfire of the Vanities*, was turned into a film.

(D) He first worked as a journalist for top American newspapers like *The Washington Post* and the *New York Herald Tribune*, winning awards for his stories.

(E) The media liked Wolfe's writing style because he did not always tell the truth as a journalist should.

Check-up

A. Choose the correct answers.

1. What should you do when answering a vocabulary question?
   (A) Eliminate answer choices that contain a synonym of the word in question.
   (B) Choose the answer choice that has a synonym of a word near the word in question.
   (C) Eliminate answer choices that contain a correct but out-of-context synonym of the word in question.
   (D) Choose the answer choice that contains the opposite meaning of the word in question.

2. When answering a reference question, you should
   (A) substitute other referents for the referent in question to find which one makes the most sense.
   (B) substitute synonyms for the words around the referent to find which one makes the most sense.
   (C) substitute antonyms for the referent to find which one makes the most sense.
   (D) substitute the answer choices in for the referent to find which one makes the most sense.

Key Vocabulary Practice

B. Fill in the blanks with the correct words.

real	awards	press	captured	storyline
imagination	fiction	prizes	newspapers	run free

1. Walt Disney used his _____ to create characters like Mickey Mouse.
2. The film version of Ghandi's life has an interesting _____.
3. Pinocchio is a wooden puppet that is turned into a(n) _____ boy by a fairy.
4. Leo Tolstoy was one of Russia's greatest _____ writers.
5. Saddam Hussein was _____ by US forces on December 13, 2003.
6. The Academy _____ are a big event in the American film industry.
7. At the end of each academic year, _____ are given to top students and scholars.
8. *The Guardian* is one of the most respected _____ in England.
9. Many animal lovers do not like zoos because animals are not allowed to _____.
10. The _____ are responsible for giving us accurate daily news.

[08] Environment

Getting Ready to Read

A. Learn the words.

Key Vocabulary

dependence	the state of relying on someone or something
non-renewable	not able to be recreated or restored
comfortable	satisfactory; not unpleasant
geothermal	pertaining to heat generated by the Earth
long run	an indefinite time period, generally lengthy

TOEFL® Vocabulary

pollutants	agents that contaminate
restore	to make something the same as it was before
incentive	a reason to do something
extract	to take out
principle	main; primary

B. Learn the question types.

TOEFL® Question Types

Factual Information

The author's description of X mentions which of the following?
According to the passage, X occurred because
According to the author, X did Y because

- Incorrect answer choices may repeat unrelated details from the passage.
- Incorrect answer choices may include information not mentioned in the passage.

Negative Factual Information

According to the passage, which of the following is NOT true of X?
The author's description of X mentions all of the following EXCEPT

- Incorrect answer choices include details that are directly stated in the passage.
- Correct answer choices may include details that are directly stated in the passage but not in connection to the topic of the question.

C. Read the passage. Number each paragraph with the correct main idea or purpose.

1. An explanation of how geothermal heating works
2. How geothermal heating can save money
3. The reasons why we should find alternate energy sources

Geothermal Heating

___ Our dependence on fossil fuels is a huge problem. Fossil fuels emit pollutants into the air. And they are non-renewable. That means that once you use them, they can't be restored. That is, we can't create any more. Finally, like all scarce resources, they are expensive. So we have the incentive to find other energy sources.

___ One option comes from the Earth. Under the surface of the Earth, there is a natural source of heat. We can extract this heat and use it in our homes. We do this by putting a heat pump deep in the Earth. It pumps heat from the Earth into our homes in the winter. The energy is clean and it never runs out.

___ Unfortunately, you cannot get enough heat from the Earth to maintain a comfortable temperature in your home. You still have to use another source, such as electricity. However, if you use geothermal as your principal heating source, your second source of energy will not be exerted as much. This will bring down your heating costs during the winter months. Though geothermal heating systems are expensive to install, they save money in the long run.

D. Complete the summary notes by filling in the blanks.

Topic: _____

Problems with fossil fuels: Fossil fuels _____. Fossil fuels are non-renewable so _____. Fossil fuels are expensive like _____.

Geothermal heating: The Earth is a _____. We can extract heat by _____ deep in the Earth. It is a clean energy source and it

_____.

Financial considerations: Need to have _____. Using geothermal as your _____ will save money. Geothermal heating systems are _____. Geothermal heating systems _____.

E. Choose the correct answers.

1. Which of the following is NOT mentioned as a reason to find alternate fuel sources?

(A) Fossil fuels pollute the air.

(B) Fossil fuels are inefficient.

2. According to the passage, which of the following is true of geothermal heating?

(A) It heats your house to a comfortable temperature.

(B) It uses heat from the Earth.

3. Which of the following is NOT mentioned as a reason to use geothermal heating?

(A) It is cheap to install.

(B) It will save you money in the long run.

4. According to the passage, which of the following is a drawback of geothermal heating?

(A) It's expensive to install.

(B) It's expensive to run.

TOEFL® Vocabulary Practice

F. Fill in the blanks with the correct words.

pollutants	restore	incentive	extract	principle

1. Catching criminals is the _____ job of a police officer.

2. Oil rigs _____ oil from the Earth.

3. The threat of losing one's job provides the _____ to work harder.

4. Smog is the result of _____ in the air.

5. A good rainfall will _____ water levels after a drought.

Practice

A. Learn the words.

Key Vocabulary

greenhouse gas	gas that absorbs and stores the Sun's heat
grasp	to understand
carbon footprint	an individual's impact on the environment throughout their lifetime
consumption	use of resources
counter	to cancel out

TOEFL® Vocabulary

implication	significance; consequence
minimize	to make as small as possible
assess	to evaluate
exceed	to go beyond
offset	to counterbalance or compensate for

Reading Passage

B. Read the passage and underline the key information.

Carbon Footprints

Humans are doing a lot of damage to the Earth. Our lifestyles rely on certain technologies. And many of these technologies require power. The sources of that power emit greenhouse gases. These gases pollute the air. Polluting the air has serious implications. For one thing, it's not healthy to breathe polluted air. In addition, greenhouse gases cause the Earth's temperature to rise. This causes changes in the climate. Climate change is responsible for extreme weather like floods, droughts, and storms.

Sometimes the problem seems overwhelming. Individuals wonder what they can do. One way to grasp the subject is through the idea of a carbon footprint. This is the amount of greenhouse gases we are each responsible for. So, instead of feeling overwhelmed by the enormity of the problem, we can do something. We can reduce our carbon footprint.

How can we change our lifestyles to minimize our carbon footprints? First, we can assess our current level of consumption. Then, we can explore ways to reduce it. If we have to drive, we can set a limit to how much we drive. Then, we may not exceed this limit. But what if we do exceed it?

The other positive thing we can do is offset our carbon footprint. This means doing positive things for the Earth to counter the negative things we do. For example, we can plant trees. Trees filter the air and also serve as an energy source.

C. **Choose the correct answers.**

1. The word this in the passage refers to
   (A) increased temperature   (B) greenhouse gases

2. Which of the following was NOT mentioned as a result of greenhouse gases?
   (A) Health problems   (B) Increased UV rays

3. The word current in the passage is closest in meaning to
   (A) flow   (B) present

4. According to the passage, what can people do to reduce their carbon footprint if they can't change their lifestyles?
   (A) to offset their footprint by doing something positive
   (B) to assess their level of consumption

TOEFL® Vocabulary Practice

D. **Fill in the blanks with the correct words.**

| implications | minimize | assess | exceed | offset |

1. Governments can _____ the burden of rising oil prices by issuing checks to the poor.

2. In order to save money one must _____ expenditures.

3. The Equal Rights Amendment had important _____ for racial minorities.

4. Managers _____ each employee's performance to determine if they deserve a pay raise.

5. It's possible to get a speeding ticket if you _____ the speed limit.

Read the passage.

Water Pollution

Water is a precious resource. Humans and animals cannot live without it. Plants would not grow without it. Adding pollutants to the water supply, then, can have serious implications. Many people have limited water supplies. If their principal water supply contains pollutants, they could get sick. This is a serious problem in many developing countries.

Water is a renewable resource. Supplies are naturally restored through the water cycle. Water evaporates into the air. Then it condenses in clouds. Then it falls back to the Earth as rain or snow. ■ 1) Then it makes its way back to the rivers, streams, ponds, and oceans. ■ 2) And the cycle starts over again when it evaporates. ■ 3) As you can see, you cannot create more water. ■ 4) Nor can you get rid of water. It just keeps getting recycled. However, once water becomes polluted, it is difficult to extract the pollutants. They will remain in the water through the stages of the water cycle. It is therefore important to take the initiative to minimize the amount of pollutants that get in the water supply.

In order to reduce water pollution, we must assess its sources. Farms are a major source of pollution. We use different chemicals on our crops to protect them from insects and pests. But when it rains, the water carries the chemicals. Then the chemicals get into the water system. But we need to grow crops. So we have to find chemicals that don't harm the water. The government has made laws to limit the use of dangerous chemicals. Farmers cannot exceed these levels. The same is true of factories and other sources of pollutants. These are called point-source pollution because we know where it comes from. It comes from a definite source. The other type is non-point-source pollution. This is where pollutants get into the water supply from a variety of sources. We cannot pinpoint where these types of pollutants come from exactly, so they are difficult to regulate.

Water pollution is highly regulated now that we understand it. But that does not mean that it is no longer a problem.

Choose the correct answers.

1. The word precious in the passage is closest in meaning to

(A) adored

(B) favorite

(C) valuable

(D) expensive

2. The word they in the paragraph 1 refers to

(A) pollutants

(B) water supplies

(C) countries

(D) people

3. Which of the following is true of water?

(A) It is non-renewable.
(B) It is essential for life.
(C) It is running out.
(D) It is lost in the water cycle.

4. Which of the following is NOT part of the water cycle?

(A) evaporation
(B) condensation
(C) restoration
(D) rain

5. Look at the four squares (■) that indicate where the following sentence could be added to the passage.

This is called precipitation.

Where would the sentence best fit?

(A) Square 1
(B) Square 2
(C) Square 3
(D) Square 4

6. Complete the table by selecting the appropriate pollution source from the answer choices and matching them to the type of water pollution. TWO of the answer choices will not be used. **This question is worth 3 points.**

(A) Factories
(B) Clouds
(C) Farms
(D) Trees
(E) General garbage
(F) Various contaminants from water sports and commercial boating
(G) Oil spills

Point-source pollution

• _____
• _____
• _____

Non-point-source pollution

• _____
• _____

Check-up

A. Choose the correct answers.

1. What should you do when answering a factual information question?
   (A) Eliminate answer choices that include details mentioned directly in the passage.
   (B) Choose the answer choice with details from the passage that are not related to the question.
   (C) Eliminate answer choices that include information not mentioned in the passage.
   (D) Choose the answer choice with details unrelated to the passage.

2. When answering a negative factual information question, you should
   (A) eliminate answer choices that contradict information from the passage.
   (B) look carefully for details that are mentioned in the passage but not in relation to what the question asks.
   (C) choose the answer choice that supports the main idea of the passage.
   (D) eliminate details that are mentioned in the passage but not in relation to what the question asks.

Key Vocabulary Practice

B. Fill in the blanks with the correct words.

dependence	non-renewable	comfortable	geothermal	long run
greenhouse gases	grasp		carbon footprint	consumption	counter

1. _____ are responsible for global warming.

2. Economics majors have a good _____ on how the economy works.

3. The music industry is looking for ways to _____ the effects of free downloading.

4. If you are not rich, but not poor, you are _____.

5. Re-insulating a house may be expensive, but saves money in the _____.

6. _____ heating systems rely on heat naturally generated by the Earth.

7. The rate of _____ in the West is not sustainable.

8. Fossil fuels and nuclear power are _____ resources.

9. Using mass transit is one way to cut down on one's _____.

10. Social welfare programs should discourage people from developing a _____ on them.

[09] Health and Psychology

Getting Ready to Read

A. Learn the words.

Key Vocabulary

respiratory	having to do with breathing
circulation	the flow of blood through the body
prevalence	how often something occurs
addictive	causing users to easily become dependent
stimulant	something that speeds up bodily processes

TOEFL® Vocabulary

trigger	to cause; to make happen
exposure	the act of subjecting someone to something
incidence	the rate at which something occurs
reluctance	the state of being hesitant; the state of not wanting to do something
tense	feeling mental strain

B. Learn the question types.

TOEFL® Question Types

Sentence Simplification
Which of the following best expresses the essential information in the highlighted sentence? *Incorrect* answers change the meaning in important ways or leave out essential information.

- Incorrect answer choices may contain important details from the highlighted sentence but use them differently.
- Incorrect answer choices may contradict the message of the highlighted sentence.

C. Read the passage. Number each paragraph with the correct main idea or purpose.

1. The effects of second hand smoke
2. Why smoking tobacco is bad for one's health
3. Why smokers continue to smoke
4. Conclusion that people shouldn't smoke

The Effects of Smoking

___ The fact that smoking tobacco is bad for your health is well known. Lung cancer and numerous other diseases of the respiratory system are triggered by tobacco smoking. It's also bad for the heart, the brain, and for blood circulation.

___ Smoking affects more than just the smoker. Exposure to second-hand smoke can be harmful to others. There is a higher incidence of respiratory problems among children whose parents smoke than children of non-smokers. It also seems that children of smokers do not perform as well in school.

___ So, people who don't smoke shouldn't start. And people who do smoke should quit. Even though smoking's prevalence is decreasing, people continue to smoke.

___ People's reluctance to quit smoking lies in the fact that it is addictive. This is another effect that smoking has. The body becomes dependent on the drug. People begin to think that smoking relaxes them. The truth is, smoking is a stimulant. It does not relax people. It does, however, satisfy a craving. So, the person is tricked into thinking that the drug has relaxed them. But if they weren't addicted to smoking, they would not have been tense to begin with.

D. Complete the summary by filling in the blanks.

Topic:	_____
Introduction:	Smoking is _____. Diseases of the respiratory system are _____. Also bad for the _____.
Second-hand smoke:	Is bad, too. Children of smokers have _____. Children of smokers _____.
What to do:	People _____ smoking. Smokers _____. Though smoking is _____, people still smoke.
Why people smoke:	Smoking is hard to quit _____. Smokers think that _____, but _____.

E. Choose the correct answers.

1. Which of the following best expresses the essential information in the highlighted sentence? Incorrect answers change the meaning in important ways or leave out essential information.

Lung cancer and numerous other diseases of the respiratory system are triggered by tobacco smoking.

(A) Smoking causes various respiratory diseases.
(B) Certain respiratory diseases are made worse by smoking.

2. Which of the following best expresses the essential information in the highlighted sentence? Incorrect answers change the meaning in important ways or leave out essential information.

There is a higher incidence of respiratory problems among children whose parents smoke than children of non-smokers.

(A) More respiratory diseases are found in parents of smokers than non-smokers.

(B) Children of smokers have more breathing problems than children of non-smokers.

TOEFL® Vocabulary Practice

F. Fill in the blanks with the correct words.

triggered	exposure	incidence	reluctance	tense

1. The _____ of autism has increased in recent years.

2. Some people show _____ when asked to move for work.

3. It is a good idea to take a vacation and relax if you are feeling too _____.

4. The Stock Market Crash of 1929 _____ the Great Depression.

5. _____ to UV rays can cause skin cancer.

Practice

A. Learn the words.

Key Vocabulary

applied	practical; not theoretical
therapy	treatment
psychiatrist	a medical doctor specializing in mental disorders
bound	obligated
abuse	misuse; to use for ill purpose

TOEFL® Vocabulary

psychology	the study of the mind and of behavior
hypothesis	an educated guess
validity	the degree to which something is valid or credible
code	a set of standards
ethics	rules or guidelines pertaining to what is moral

Reading Passage

B. Read the passage and underline the key information.

What Is Psychology?

Psychology is the study of the mind and of behavior. It seeks to understand how the mind works. It also tries to understand why people behave the way they do. There are many areas of psychology. The broadest are academic and applied.

Academic psychology is involved in research. There are many areas of research. In general, the scientific method is used to answer questions. These questions are about the mind and behavior. A researcher starts with a hypothesis. He or she then designs an experiment to prove or disprove it. The results are published. Then the validity of the findings can be reviewed by others.

Applied psychology uses the findings of the research. It uses them to help people. Both psychologists and psychiatrists work in this field. There is one major difference. Psychiatrists are medical doctors. They can give medicine to patients. Both assess patients and try to help them. Treatment options vary. Sometimes different types of therapy are used. Sometimes medicine can help. Often, both are used together.

All mental health workers are bound by a code of ethics. They have a certain power over patients. They must not abuse this power. Trust is very important in their relationship with patients. So they cannot repeat what patients tell them. Only if the patient allows it can they repeat it. Further, all actions must be in the best interest of the patient. This code of ethics is very important. Without it, more harm than good could come out of therapy.

C. Choose the correct answers.

1. Which of the following best expresses the essential information in the highlighted sentence? Incorrect answers change the meaning in important ways or leave out essential information.

   It also tries to understand why people behave the way they do.

   (A) It also tries to understand motivations for behaviors.
   (B) It also explains why people think like they do.

2. Which of the following best expresses the essential information in the highlighted sentence? Incorrect answers change the meaning in important ways or leave out essential information.

   Then the validity of the findings can be reviewed by others.

   (A) Then others can learn from the results.
   (B) Then others can check to make sure they're valid.

3. Which of the following is NOT mentioned as part of the scientific method?

   (A) Prescribing medicine to help mentally ill patients
   (B) Doing experiments to test hypotheses

4. According to the passage, what is the difference between a psychiatrist and psychologist?

   (A) Psychologists try to help patients, while psychiatrists do research.
   (B) Psychiatrists are licensed to prescribe medicine to patients.

TOEFL® Vocabulary Practice

D. Fill in the blanks with the correct words.

psychology	hypothesis	validity	code	ethics

1. People who are interested in the mind study _____.

2. It is important to assess a study's _____ before jumping to any conclusions.

3. The _____ that smoking causes cancer has been proven many times.

4. A person's _____ will determine what they believe is right or wrong.

5. The boy scouts have a(n) _____ that guides their behavior when outdoors.

Read the passage.

The Mind and Body

We know when we are sick because we get symptoms. If our bodies are sick, we get physical symptoms. If our minds are sick, we have mental symptoms. But sometimes we have mental problems that trigger physical symptoms. For example, if we are very tense, we might get a headache. And sometimes much more serious problems can develop.

Throughout history, many people have investigated the mind-body connection to illness. Many doctors including Greek and Islamic doctors noticed it. They had the hypothesis that mind and body affect each other. They did a simple study to test it. They found that people whose minds were healthy tended to have healthy bodies. And people with mental problems tended to have physical problems.

■ 1) Today, there is no doubt that our minds can make us physically sick. When we can't find a disease to explain physical symptoms, we must look to psychology. But some people show reluctance when asked to speak with their doctors about emotional issues. They believe that their symptoms are physical in nature, so they must be physically ill. They should be given medicine. ■ 2) The idea that the problem is in their minds can be insulting. But it needn't be. If one's emotional state is causing physical illness, it does not mean that the person is crazy. Nor does it mean that he or she is imagining things. The symptoms are very real. And their causes are very real. There is no question as to the validity of the illness. ■ 3)

Some mind-body disorders can be quite serious. ■ 4) An example is anorexia. This is an eating disorder. Some say that a cause is the exposure of young people to unrealistically thin role models in the media. Whatever the cause, it is a mental disorder. But it shows itself through physical symptoms. Patients starve themselves, sometimes to death. They do this because they want to look a certain way. And when they look in the mirror, their perception is distorted. Even if they are very thin, they think they look fat. Clearly, low self-esteem is a huge factor. The incidence of anorexia is growing.

Choose the correct answers.

1. The word study in paragraph 2 is closest in meaning to

(A) schoolwork
(B) examination
(C) office
(D) subject

2. The word it in paragraph 2 refers to

(A) mind

(B) body

(C) study

(D) hypothesis

3. Look at the four squares (■) that indicate where the following sentence could be added to the passage.

The only question is of the source of the illness.

Where would the sentence best fit?

(A) Square 1

(B) Square 2

(C) Square 3

(D) Square 4

4. Which of the following best expresses the essential information in the highlighted sentence? Incorrect answers change the meaning in important ways or leave out essential information.

Some say that a cause is the exposure of young people to unrealistically thin models in the media.

(A) It is thought that models have a higher incidence of anorexia.

(B) It is thought that anorexics want to be models.

(C) Some think the media features unrealistic models.

(D) Some think that the media creates unrealistic standards.

5. Which of the following is NOT true of anorexia according to the passage?

(A) It has no physical symptoms.

(B) It can result in death.

(C) It is caused by low self-esteem.

(D) It is becoming more common.

6. An introductory sentence for a brief summary of the passage is provided below. Complete the summary by selecting the THREE answer choices that express the most important ideas in the passage. Some sentences do not belong in the summary because they express ideas that are not presented in the passage or are minor ideas in the passage. **This question is worth 2 points.**

The mind–body connection is complex.

(A) Unhealthy minds cause no physical symptoms.

(B) Doctors have recently noticed this phenomenon.

(C) People with healthy minds have healthy bodies.

(D) Physical symptoms of mental problems are very real.

(E) Anorexia is a common mind–body disorder.

Check-up

A. Choose the correct answer.

1. When answering a sentence simplification question, you should
    (A) eliminate answer choices that paraphrase the highlighted sentence.
    (B) eliminate answer choices that use important details from the highlighted sentence to convey a different meaning.
    (C) eliminate answer choices that use important details from the highlighted sentence to convey the same meaning in fewer words.
    (D) eliminate answer choices that use some important details to summarize the main idea of the highlighted sentence.

2. What should you do when answering a sentence simplification question?
    (A) Eliminate answer choices that paraphrase the highlighted sentence.
    (B) Eliminate answer choices that use some important details to summarize the main idea of the highlighted sentence.
    (C) Eliminate answer choices that contradict the message of the highlighted sentence.
    (D) Eliminate answer choices that use important details from the highlighted sentence to convey the same meaning in fewer words.

Key Vocabulary Practice

B. Fill in the blanks with the correct words.

respiratory	circulation	prevalence	addictive	stimulant
applied	therapy	psychiatrists	bound	abused

1. The _____ of many diseases often decreases once its major cause is identified.
2. Caffeine is _____. Once you start drinking coffee, it's very hard to give up.
3. _____ deal with mentally ill patients.
4. Unlike theoretical linguistics, _____ linguistics is concerned primarily with teaching language.
5. Poor _____ can cause muscle cramps.
6. _____ problems are common in areas with air pollution.
7. Caffeine is a(n) _____. It causes your heart to beat faster.
8. Some psychologists use hypnosis as a form of _____.
9. Doctors are _____ by the Hippocratic Oath.
10. If a friend tells someone about your secrets then they have _____ your trust.

[10] Technology

Getting Ready to Read

A. Learn the words.

text	written words
link	a word in electronic format that can be clicked on to open another document
media	means of communication
publisher	one who prepares and prints books and other literature for sale
electronically	via computers

TOEFL® Vocabulary

capable	able to
distinction	difference
equivalent	one that is the same as
version	a variant of something
distribution	the act of making something available for use

B. Learn the question types.

TOEFL® Question Types

Inference
Which of the following can be inferred about X?
The author of the passage implies that X
Which of the following can be inferred from paragraph X about Y?

- Incorrect answer choices may include an inference that is irrelevant to the passage.
- Incorrect answer choices may include an inference that is relevant but not supported by information in the passage.

Rhetorical Purpose
The author discusses X in paragraph Y in order to
The author uses X as an example of

- Incorrect answer choices may include a false or inaccurate purpose according to the information in the passage.
- Incorrect answer choices may include a purpose that is relevant to the passage but not to the words or actions asked about in the question.

C. Read the passage. Number each paragraph with the correct main idea or purpose.

> 1. How storage space is saved with e-books
> 2. What an e-book is
> 3. How e-books simplify distribution
> 4. How e-books save time
> 5. How e-books help people with difficulty reading

E-books

___ These days it seems that everything is going digital. Books are no exception. The e-book was designed to take the place of the printed book. It is a hand-held device. Text appears on a screen, just like a computer.

___ There are several advantages to the e-book. For one thing, it takes up less space. E-books are capable of storing hundreds of books. Therefore, readers will no longer need bookshelves to store all of their books.

___ Another distinction between the e-book and normal books is that it is like a computer. Users can search for certain words in a book, or links to other texts can be included. This can make research less time consuming.

___ Readers with difficulty reading will note another important difference between books and their digital media equivalent. They can change the text size to make it easier to read. Further, a text-to-speech version of the software can be added so that they can listen instead of reading.

___ From the publisher's point of view, distribution is made easier. Books are easy to replicate. The need for paper and ink is eliminated. And books don't have to be shipped as they can be sent electronically.

D. Complete the summary by filling in the blanks.

Topic:	_____
Space-saving advantage:	Can store _____ in one e-book. Don't need _____.
Time-saving advantage:	E-books have same _____. Can _____ _____. Can access other _____.
Accessibility advantage:	Readers with difficulty reading can _____. Can also use software that _____.
Distribution advantage:	Easier for _____. Books are _____ _____ and don't require _____. Books can _____.

E. Choose the correct answers.

1. The author uses links as an example of

(A) an area where e-books need to be improved

(B) an advantage offered by e-books

2. Which of the following can be inferred about e-books?

(A) They would only be useful for researching.

(B) Any genre of writing could be made available.

3. Why does the author mention text-to-speech software?

(A) To show how e-books can make literature more accessible

(B) To give an alternative to e-books for visually impaired people

4. Which of the following can be inferred about e-books?

(A) They would make it easier for authors to get published.

(B) Books would be cheaper in digital format.

TOEFL® Vocabulary Practice

F. Fill in the blanks with the correct words.

| capable | distinction | equivalent | version | distribution |

1. The metric _____ of one cup is 250 milliliters.

2. The 2005 _____ of the film *War of the Worlds* featured Tom Cruise.

3. _____ is often handled by a middleman between the manufacturer and the seller.

4. It is important to be aware of the _____ between fact and fiction.

5. Some cars are _____ of reaching speeds of up to 250 miles per hour.

Practice

A. Learn the words.

Key Vocabulary

upgrade	to make better; to make more up-to-date
biodegradable	able to decay or breakdown
eco-friendly	not damaging the environment
toxic	poisonous
motherboard	the main circuit board of a computer

TOEFL® Vocabulary

corporate	pertaining to corporations
transport	the movement of goods from one place to another
marginal	not significant
item	a thing
previous	occurring before

Reading Passage

B. Read the passage and underline the key information.

Eco-friendly Computers

Computers are now part of our everyday lives. And they keep getting better. As they do, many people upgrade. That is, when a better product comes out, they get rid of their old one and replace it. The problem with this trend is that it creates a lot of waste. Corporate interests demand that consumers continually update their systems. This often results in a lot of waste. The solution is biodegradable computers.

In many ways computers can be seen as eco-friendly. They cut down on the amount of paper we need to use. That means we cut down less trees. Information can be shipped electronically. We don't have to transport it by air, land, or sea. The amount of power it takes to run a computer is marginal. But the machines are made from toxic materials. They are not recyclable and they take up room in landfills.

A company called MicroPro began working on a solution in 1992. It has since developed an eco-friendly computer. Items such as keyboards and monitors are made of wood and other biodegradable materials. That means that you can bury them in the ground and the Earth will break them down. The computer itself is reusable. Previous computers allowed you to upgrade. But at some point you would have to replace the whole unit. This is because the technology improves so fast. But with MicroPro you can replace the motherboard. You don't have to buy a completely new computer. The materials are also recyclable.

C. Choose the correct answers.

1. Which of the following can be inferred from paragraph 1 about corporations?

(A) They charge too much for upgrades to their systems.

(B) They make money by continually improving technology.

2. Which of the following best expresses the essential information in the highlighted sentence? Incorrect answers change the meaning in important ways or leave out essential information.

Items such as keyboards and monitors are made of wood and other biodegradable materials.

(A) Peripherals are made of materials that break down.

(B) Wooden keyboards are more eco-friendly.

3. Why does the author mention the motherboard in paragraph 3?

(A) As an example of a biodegradable feature of the computer

(B) To show how the computer creates less waste than conventional computers

TOEFL® Vocabulary Practice

D. Fill in the blanks with the correct words.

corporate	transport	marginal	items	previous

1. The cost of _____ is a significant part of the price.

2. The cost of running an awareness campaign is _____ compared to the money it will save.

3. _____ tax rates are low to attract international businesses.

4. Each year new car models come out that feature various improvements on _____ models.

5. You can find various _____ for sale at flea markets.

Read the passage.

Wireless

Wi-Fi is a type of technology. It creates networks. These networks are wireless. Computers can communicate with one another without the use of wires. Internet connections can be made without wires. People can make phone calls over the Internet. The telephone wires are not used. Such items as TVs and DVD players can be connected to networks using Wi-Fi technology. Wi-Fi technologies were introduced in 1997. Since then several versions have come out. Each one is an improvement on the previous one.

How is this possible? Wireless devices have to be capable of making a connection. They would all have to use the same technology. If one company uses one type of technology, another must use its equivalent. That's the only way they can connect to the same network. So, different companies must work together to set standards. That way their different devices can work on the same network. The Wi-Fi Alliance sets these standards.

Wi-Fi is now common in corporate environments. People working in different locations can communicate easily. Distribution of tasks is simpler. People can work faster. There are fewer problems caused by delays. And the more access points, the more efficient the whole network is.

Hot spots are starting to appear in more places. These are areas where Wi-Fi is available for free. Anyone who happens to be in the area can use it. They just have to have a Wi-Fi certified device. These hot spots might be a cafe, a hotel, an airport, or even an entire city. Some cities provide free wireless Internet access.

Another good thing about Wi-Fi is cost. It gets rid of the need for cables. These can be costly to install. The cost of installing a wireless local area network is marginal in comparison. Wi-Fi also makes it easier to expand existing networks.

Wi-Fi technology has changed the way we do business. It has also changed the way we live our lives. The Internet is more accessible than ever. And we can easily network our computers with others. The Internet is now part of our everyday lives.

Choose the correct answers.

1. Why does the author mention the Wi-Fi Alliance?

   (A) To show the impact that Wi-Fi technology has had on society
   (B) To give an example of a group that has formed to support Wi-Fi
   (C) To show how one can go about obtaining a Wi-Fi connection
   (D) To explain how a problem with Wi-Fi technology is solved

2. The word set in paragraph 2 is closest in meaning to

    (A) place   (B) establish

    (C) harden   (D) vanish

3. The word it in paragraph 4 refers to

    (A) Wi-Fi   (B) the area

    (C) the person   (D) the device

4. Where might one find a hotspot?

    (A) At a cafe   (B) At a hotel

    (C) At an airport   (D) All of the above

5. What can be inferred from the passage about Wi-Fi?

    (A) It will soon be replaced with better technology.

    (B) When cables get better and cheaper it will become obsolete.

    (C) It will eventually make cabled connections obsolete.

    (D) It will be feasible once companies agree on standards.

6. Complete the table below by selecting the appropriate phrases from the answer choices and matching them to the correct heading. TWO of the answer choices will not be used. **This question is worth 3 points.**

Wi-Fi

    (A) Became available in 1997

    (B) Costly to install

    (C) Limits communication

    (D) Older technology

    (E) Not accessible to most devices

    (F) Makes business more efficient

    (G) Requires industry standards

- _____
- _____
- _____

Cabled connection

- _____
- _____

Check-up

A. Choose the correct answers.

1. When answering an inference question, you should
   (A) eliminate answer choices that contain inferences related to but not supported by information in the passage.
   (B) eliminate answer choices that contain statements clearly stated in the passage.
   (C) eliminate answer choices that contain inferences that are relevant to the main idea of the passage.
   (D) eliminate answer choices that contain inferences based on information not found in the passage.

2. What should you do when answering a rhetorical purpose question?
   (A) Eliminate answer choices that present a purpose related to the words or actions asked about in the question.
   (B) Select an answer choice that presents a purpose related to the passage but not the question asked.
   (C) Eliminate answer choices that present a purpose related to the passage but not to the words or actions asked about in the question.
   (D) Select an answer choice that presents a purpose not related to the words or actions asked about in the question.

Key Vocabulary Practice

B. Fill in the blanks with the correct words.

text	links	media	publishers	electronically
upgrade	biodegradable	eco-friendly	toxic	motherboard

1. Email allows us to send messages and pictures _____.
2. Television, newspapers, and magazines are all types of _____.
3. Aspiring writers should send their work to several _____ for consideration.
4. You can put food scraps in the garden because they are _____.
5. Pregnant women should avoid _____ fumes.
6. Environmentally conscious people choose only _____ products.
7. Many websites contain _____ to other websites that might be of interest.
8. When your software becomes outdated it is time to _____.
9. Computers display _____ in a variety of fonts, sizes, and colors.
10. The _____ is the most important component of a computer.

[11] Global Perspectives

Getting Ready to Read

A. Learn the words.

Key Vocabulary

refugee	a person who leaves their country because they are in danger
oppressed	to be the victim of cruelty or injustice; to be weighed down
prison	the place people who break the law are kept; a jail
distressing	upsetting; causing worry and stress
urgently	done immediately or quickly due to crisis

TOEFL® Vocabulary

abandon	to leave; to give up; to desert
politics	the art or science of government
integration	the act of blending or mixing; the act of becoming part of
contend	to struggle, strive, or deal with
convenience	something that makes things easier or more comfortable

B. Learn the question types.

TOEFL® Question Types

Insert Text

Look at the four squares [■] that indicate where the following sentence could be added to the passage.

[You will see a sentence in bold.]

Where would the sentence best fit?

- Incorrect answer choices may not fit with the logical sequence of ideas in the passage.
- Incorrect answer choices may not contain the correct grammatical structure to fit in with sentences before or after the square.
- Incorrect answer choices may contain inappropriate transitional words or phrases.

C. **Read the passage. Number each paragraph with the correct main idea or purpose.**

> 1. Information on what refugees must do to be safe
> 2. Details on the lives of refugees in a new country
> 3. The meaning of the word refugee
> 4. Information about what some governments think about refugees
> 5. Information on why refugees have to run away

Refugees

___ Refugees are people who leave their home country because they are being oppressed and feel in great danger. If they stay they may be thrown in prison. They may also be killed.

___ They have to abandon their homes. ■ 1) They have to leave their jobs. ■ 2) They have to run away to a new country. ■ 3) They often have to leave without their families. ■ 4) If they don't, they could die.

___ This is usually because the government of their country does not like their politics. Sometimes it is because the government does not like their religion.

___ Life in a new country can be distressing for refugees. ■ 5) Integration into a new culture is not always easy. ■ 6) Refugees also have a lot to contend with. ■ 7) They have to find a place to live. They have to look for work. Often they have no money. This is because they had to leave their own country urgently. They have had no time to plan for a new life. ■ 8)

___ Another problem they face is that sometimes the governments in their new home do not believe they were in danger. They think these people only moved home out of convenience. They think the refugees left their own country because it is poor. They believe refugees are looking for a better life in a rich country.

D. **Complete the summary by filling in the blanks.**

Topic:	_____
Introduction:	_____ are people who _____ because they are _____. Stay and may be thrown in _____ or _____.
Leaving:	Have to _____ their _____, _____, and families and _____ to a new country.
Reasons:	Usually because _____ don't like their _____ _____.
Integration:	Not easy and life can be _____ because refugees have lot to _____ with. Have to find home and _____ and often no _____. Had to leave home _____ and had _____.
Governments:	Problem is they think refugees are not in _____. They think refugees moved for _____ because own country is _____. Believe they seek better _____ in a _____ country.

E. Choose the correct answers.

1. Look at the four squares (■) in paragraph 2 that indicate where the following sentence could be added.

   They have no choice about these things.

   Where would the sentence best fit?

   (A) Square 1   (B) Square 2
   (C) Square 3   (D) Square 4

2. The word contend in paragraph 4 is closest in meaning to

   (A) cope   (B) survive

3. Look at the four squares (■) in paragraph 4 that indicate where the following sentence could be added.

   Everything is so different, from the food to the language.

   Where would the sentence best fit?

   (A) Square 5   (B) Square 6
   (C) Square 7   (D) Square 8

4. According to the passage, many governments think refugees are liars because

   (A) they don't believe refugees are really in danger
   (B) they do not like people from strange places

TOEFL® Vocabulary Practice

F. Fill in the blanks with the correct words.

abandoned	integration	convenience	politics	contend

1. Many countries do not like the _____ of North Korea's leader, Kim Jong-il.

2. Nurses have a lot to _____ with working in hospitals with so many sick people.

3. A microwave oven is a modern _____ because it cooks food so quickly.

4. Racial _____ between black and white people in the US has taken many years.

5. Many mountaineers have _____ the ascent of Mount Everest because of bad weather.

Practice

A. Learn the words.

Key Vocabulary

environmental	relating to the Earth and nature
global warming	heating up of the Earth's atmosphere due to gas trapped therein
flood	when a heavy rainfall causes water levels to rise; a deluge; a great flow of water
halt	to stop or cease
Kyoto Protocol	a treaty signed in 1997 whereby governments agreed to reduce use of fossil fuels/greenhouse gas emissions

TOEFL® Vocabulary

vocal	spoken or outspoken; voiced; uttered
successive	one after the other; following on; sequential
conference	a meeting of many speakers talking together
assemble	to gather or meet in one place
protocol	a treaty which determines rules of conduct between parties

Reading Passage

B. Read the passage and underline the key information.

The Kyoto Protocol

The countries of the world often argue about environmental issues. ■ 1) Some are very vocal about global warming because they think it is very dangerous. ■ 2) They think that countries like the US use too many fossil fuels such as oil. ■ 3) Using too much of these fuels hurts the environment and causes global warming. ■ 4)

Global warming is changing our weather. There are more floods and storms in many places. Often, many people are killed in floods. For years, scientists have warned us that we have to use less fuel.

There have been successive meetings between leaders to figure out what to do. One of the most important conferences took place in Japan in 1997. It was held in the city of Kyoto. Leaders from many countries assembled in a meeting room there to talk about what to do. They talked a lot and then some of them agreed to try to halt global warming. They signed a document called "The Kyoto Protocol."

Some countries did not want to stop using fossil fuels and their leaders did not sign at Kyoto. They thought scientists were lying and making things sound more serious than they are. Some countries that sell oil to the rest of the world did not want to sign. They were scared their countries would become poor if people used less oil. Leaders who signed believe we can find new forms of energy. They pay scientists to find out what we can do. Many scientists believe we can use the Sun to make energy. We can also use wind or water.

C. Choose the correct answers.

1. Look at the four squares (■) in paragraph 1 that indicate where the following sentence could be added.

   When oil burns it makes gas that then becomes trapped in the Earth's atmosphere.

   Where would the sentence best fit?

   (A) Square 1   (B) Square 2
   (C) Square 3   (D) Square 4

2. The word vocal in paragraph 1 is closest in meaning to

   (A) angry   (B) talkative

3. What can be inferred from the passage about Japan?

   (A) It supported the Kyoto Protocol because the conference took place in Japan.
   (B) It was against the Kyoto Protocol because the conference took place in Japan.

4. Why does the author mention that energy can be made using sun, wind or water power?

   (A) To show that it is possible to use less fossil fuel
   (B) To show how smart scientists are

TOEFL® Vocabulary Practice

D. Fill in the blanks with the correct words.

vocal	assembled	conferences	successive	protocols

1. _____ Israeli prime ministers have been unable to make peace with the Arabs.

2. There are many medical _____ to discuss the problems of HIV/Aids.

3. On February 11, 1990 many people _____ in Cape Town to see Nelson Mandela become free after twenty-seven years in prison.

4. There are very strict _____ about using nuclear weapons because they are so dangerous.

5. If your _____ chords are cut, you will be unable to speak.

Test

Read the passage.

The United Nations

The United Nations is an international organization. It was created in 1945 after the Second World War. The name was chosen by Franklin D. Roosevelt, who was president of the US. At that time the whole world was very tired of war. Many people were killed between 1939 and 1945. They were oppressed by Nazi Germany. It was a very distressing time.

Leaders decided to work together to halt future wars. ■ **1)** That is why they created the United Nations. ■ **2)** They wanted the countries of the world to work together to keep the peace. ■ **3)** They also wanted to help the poor and stop diseases. ■ **4)** After the war, leaders had a lot to contend with. Countries had to be re-built. The United Nations was a way for everyone to help each other.

The first UN conference was held on April 25, 1945 in San Francisco. The leaders of fifty nations assembled there to decide how the UN would work. They had to decide on many different protocols for the organization. They also had to choose a leader.

The leader of the UN is called the Secretary-General. He or she is chosen to serve for five years. It is this person's job to be vocal about things the UN should do to keep world peace. The first Secretary-General was Trygve Lie of Norway. There have been eight successive leaders since 1946. In January 2007, Ban Ki-Moon of South Korea was chosen as the new Secretary-General.

Today, 192 countries are part of the UN. The organization has changed a lot over the last sixty years. It had to abandon or change many protocols. This is because world politics have also changed over time. The world is not the same place as it was in 1945. There are new problems facing the UN these days. These include environmental problems, such as global warming.

The United Nations has always tried urgently to stop wars but it has not really succeeded. It is still important to have a body like the UN because it helps world leaders communicate. This is a big convenience.

Choose the correct answers.

1. The word oppressed in paragraph 1 is closest in meaning to

(A) distressed   (B) treated badly

(C) cared for   (D) loved

2. Look at the four squares (■) in paragraph 2 that indicate where the following sentence could be added.

They wanted a way to make the world a better place.

Where would the sentence best fit?

(A) Square 1   (B) Square 2

(C) Square 3   (D) Square 4

3. All of the following are true of the United Nations EXCEPT

(A) it was formed in 1945 after the Second World War
(B) Ban Ki-Moon of Korea was the UN's first Secretary-General
(C) it has 192 member states
(D) it has had to abandon and change many protocols in the last sixty years

4. Why does the author state the current number of member states of the UN?

(A) She finds it interesting that there are more members than in 1945.
(B) She wants to show that the UN has grown in size and importance.
(C) She thinks the amount of members is too small.
(D) She is excited that the amount is close to 200 members.

5. The highlighted word This in the last paragraph refers to

(A) world leaders trying to stop wars
(B) the United Nations Organization
(C) world leaders talking to each other
(D) an organization that tries to halt wars

6. An introductory sentence for a brief summary of the passage is provided below. Complete the summary by selecting the THREE answer choices that express the most important ideas in the passage. Some sentences do not belong in the summary because they express ideas that are not presented in the passage or are minor ideas in the passage.

The United Nations is an international organization created to maintain world peace.

Answer choices

(A) The leader of the UN is called the Secretary-General and is currently Ban Ki- Moon of South Korea.
(B) Oppression by Nazi Germany caused the death and torture of millions of people leading to the formation of the UN.
(C) The UN has changed a lot in sixty years, facing new challenges such as global warming and gaining many new members.
(D) The Secretary-General of the UN serves a five year term before a new leader is chosen.
(E) It was created in 1945 after the Second World War in order to re-build countries, keep the peace, and help those in need.

Check-up

A. Choose the correct answers.

1. What should you do when answering an insert text question?

(A) Eliminate answer choices whose grammatical structure does not fit in with the sentences before and after the square.

(B) Eliminate answer choices that present ideas that form a logical progression to the ideas presented before the square.

(C) Eliminate answer choices whose grammatical structure fits in with the sentences before and after the square.

(D) Eliminate answer choices that contain appropriate transitional words or phrases.

Key Vocabulary Practice

B. Fill in the blanks with the correct words.

| distressing | Kyoto Protocol | halt | oppressed | global warming |
| flood | urgently | prison | environmental | refugees |

1. There are many _____ from Africa's war zones living in London.

2. The transplant was performed _____ because the man was about to die.

3. Alcatraz is a famous _____ on an island off the coast of San Francisco.

4. Losing a loved one is very _____ for family members.

5. The hole in the ozone layer is a serious _____ issue.

6. In December 2004, a giant wave caused a(n) _____ of water that killed thousands.

7. Police try to _____ the trade of drugs by sending dealers to prison for many years.

8. The US did not want to sign the _____ in 1997.

9. Stalin _____ the people of the USSR and they lived in fear.

10. _____ is caused by CO_2 gas trapped in the atmosphere.

[12] Theater and Sport

Getting Ready to Read

A. Learn the words.

Key Vocabulary

acting	performing in a play; playing a part
community hall	a big room where people meet for activities or important meetings
respected	to be esteemed; to be thought of as good and worthy
humorous	funny; witty; comedic
musical	a play or performance with songs

TOEFL® Vocabulary

amateur	a person who does something out of love or enjoyment, not for money
professional	something done for money or payment or something done expertly
appreciation	the act of seeing good qualities in something or someone
classical	a style based on old Greek and Roman artistic models
adaptation	something changed from its original form or made more modern

B. Learn the question types.

TOEFL® Question Types

Table

Directions: Complete the table by matching the X below.

Directions: Select the appropriate X from the answer choices and match them to Y. TWO of the answer choices will not be used. **This question is worth 3 or 4 points.**

• Incorrect answer choices may include information not related to the passage.
• Incorrect answer choices may include information that contradicts that in the passage.
• Incorrect answer choices may include information not relevant to the categories in the chart.

C. Read the passage. Number each paragraph with the correct main idea or purpose.

1. Information on what kind of plays amateurs and professional actors choose
2. Information on how many plays amateurs and professional actors perform
3. Information on where amateurs and professional actors practice
4. Why amateur theater is so popular all over the world

Amateur Theater Groups

____ Amateur theater is popular in many countries. It is a fun way for people who enjoy acting to get together and put on plays. Unlike professional theater, no one gets paid. People just do it because they have a great appreciation for theater and a love of acting. It is a great way to make friends. It is fun for the whole family.

____ Amateur theater groups usually meet in a school or community hall to practice. They are usually people who live in small towns. Professional actors meet in real theaters. They live and work in big cities like New York.

____ Amateur groups usually put on classical plays or those by famous and respected writers. They like their audience to laugh so they also often choose humorous plays. Sometimes they do adaptations or musicals. It gives them a chance to sing and dance. Professional actors like to do new plays by exciting writers and often choose more serious plays.

____ Amateur groups usually put on about one or two plays a year. This is because there is not always much time for actors to meet. They can only do so after work or on weekends. Professionals try to do more plays. The more they do, the more they get paid.

D. Complete the summary by filling in the blanks.

Topic:	_____
Introduction:	_____ theater is _____ in many countries. Unlike _____ theater, no one gets _____. People do it because they have _____ for theater and a _____. Great way to make _____ and fun for _____.
Where they meet:	Amateur _____ usually meet in a school or _____. _____ actors meet in real _____ and live and work in big _____.
The Plays:	Amateurs usually do _____ plays or those by _____. Often choose _____ plays, adaptations, or _____. Professionals do _____ plays by _____ writers and more _____ plays.
How often:	Amateurs usually do one or two _____. Only meet after work or on _____. Professionals try to do more plays.

E. Choose the correct answers.

1. Complete the table below by selecting the appropriate phrases from the answer choices and matching them to the correct heading. TWO of the answer choices will not be used. **This question is worth 3 points.**

(A) Often choose musicals or funny plays
(B) Meet in real theaters in big cities
(C) Get paid to act
(D) Only do classical plays
(E) Act for fun and appreciation
(F) Often do new plays by exciting writers
(G) In community halls or schools
(H) Do more plays to make more money
(I) Money for whole family

Amateur Theater
• _____
• _____
• _____

Professional Actors
• _____
• _____
• _____
• _____

2. Which of the following best expresses the essential information in the highlighted sentence? Incorrect answers change the meaning in important ways or leave out essential information.

They like their audience to laugh so they also often choose humorous plays.

(A) They like to laugh at the people watching so they do lots of comedies.
(B) The audience's amusement is important so they frequently select funny plays.
(C) The enjoyment of the crowd means they may only do hilarious stage work.

F. Fill in the blanks with the correct words.

amateurs	classical	appreciation	professional	adaptations

1. Maria Sharapova is a(n) _____ tennis player.

2. The world still has a great _____ for the music of Amadeus Mozart.

3. Director Kenneth Branagh has done many film _____ of Shakespeare plays.

4. All athletes start off as _____ before they are good enough to make money from playing sport.

5. In _____ times, the tragedies of playwrights Sophocles and Euripides were often performed.

Practice

A. Learn the words.

helmets	hard hats used to protect the head
goal posts	a pair of posts used to form a goal in various games
score	to get a point or points in a sport match or game
referee	the person who makes sure game rules are followed by players
whistle	a small instrument that makes a sharp sound when blown

TOEFL® Vocabulary

differentiation	the act of telling the difference between things
injury	a wound or some kind of physical damage
uniform	the same clothes worn by members of a group that shows they belong
versus	a word of Latin origin meaning "against"
neutral	not choosing a side; not taking part in a dispute or competition

Reading Passage

B. Read the passage and underline the key information.

Soccer

Soccer is the world's most popular team sport. It is called football in England. This can be confusing because Americans play a different sport that is also called football. This makes differentiation between the two sports hard for some people.

American football has different rules from soccer. It is a very physical game played with an oval-shaped brown ball. It is easier for players to get injuries because they run at each other and bump each other a lot. That is why they have to wear helmets to protect their heads.

Soccer players only wear uniforms and a soccer ball is round and black and white. Both sports have eleven players per team. Both sports have one team versus another playing for points. Soccer players try to score goals by kicking the ball into a net. American football players get points by scoring touchdowns. This is done by putting the ball down behind the other team's goal posts.

Both sports use a referee and it is his job to make sure players stick to the rules. ■ 1) The referee is neutral, which means he cannot choose sides. ■ 2) He blows a whistle when he wants the game to stop. ■ 3) He does this when someone has broken a rule. ■ 4)

When soccer players break the rules the referee can give them a yellow card. This is a warning that they have to be careful. If they break another rule, he gives them a red card. Then the player has to leave the sports field and cannot play anymore.

C. Choose the correct answers.

1. Complete the table below by selecting the appropriate phrases from the answer choices and matching them to the correct heading. TWO of the answer choices will not be used. **This question is worth 4 points.**

   (A) Uses an oval shaped ball
   (B) Points scored with touchdowns
   (C) Uses a referee
   (D) Played with eleven players
   (E) Played without uniforms
   (F) Played without helmets
   (G) Bad players get blue card
   (H) Points scored by goal in net
   (I) Called football in England

   American Football
   • _____
   • _____

   Soccer
   • _____
   • _____
   • _____

   Both sports
   • _____
   • _____

2. Look at the four squares (■) that indicate where the following sentence could be added to the passage. Where would the sentence best fit?

   A referee that favored one team over another would get in serious trouble.

   (A) Square 1   (B) Square 2
   (C) Square 3   (D) Square 4

TOEFL® Vocabulary Practice

D. Fill in the blanks with the correct words.

injuries	versus	neutral	differentiation	uniforms

1. Soldiers and policemen must always have neat _____.

2. It is hard for color-blind people to see a(n) _____ between red and green.

3. Roe _____ Wade was a very important court case in US legal history.

4. Brain _____ are very dangerous and the reason people wear helmets.

5. Switzerland has stayed _____ in all major European wars.

Test

Read the passage.

The Olympic Games

The Olympic Games are an international event. Athletes compete in many different sports to win medals. They are held every four years in different countries. The 2004 games were held in Athens, Greece and the 2008 games were held in Beijing, China.

The first Olympic Games were held in classical times. ■ 1) They began in the city of Olympia in 776 BCE. ■ 2) At that time, runners from all over Greece took part in many different races and other athletic events. ■ 3) Some of the races were long and hard. Athletes often got injuries. ■ 4)

The athletes competed naked. Greeks had a great appreciation for the human body. They respected the beauty of athlete's bodies. This is why they did not wear uniforms. No women took part. It was only for men. The prize for winning an event was a crown of olive leaves. In 394 CE these games were stopped.

In 1894, a Frenchman called Pierre De Coubertin decided to bring the Olympic Games back. He organized a meeting in Paris to decide which sports should be part of the games. Some people wanted sports like football with referees blowing whistles. Most people only wanted running and other athletic sports.

The first modern Olympics were held in Athens in 1896. There was much differentiation between the modern Olympics and the ancient Greek games. Many adaptations were made. Firstly, it was no longer Greeks versus other Greeks. There were athletes from many different countries who took part. Secondly, the athletes did not compete naked. They wore uniforms to show what countries they were from. Thirdly, they won medals for the first time and not olive crowns. A gold medal was given for the first prize.

There were also many more events like shooting, tennis, weightlifting, and swimming. There were nine different sports and 143 different events. Only 241 athletes took part in the 1896 Olympics. All the athletes were amateurs. They did not get paid.

The Olympics have changed a lot since 1896. These days thousands of athletes take part. There were 10,000 athletes at the Athens games in 2004. More than half of them were women. Professional athletes can also take part now.

Choose the correct answers.

1. The word injuries in paragraph 2 is closest in meaning to

   (A) wounds
   (C) cramps

   (B) praise
   (D) sickness

2. Look at the four squares that indicate where the following sentence could be added to the passage. Where would the sentence best fit?

   That is why they are called the Olympic Games to this day.

   (A) Square 1
   (C) Square 3

   (B) Square 2
   (D) Square 4

3. The highlighted word It in paragraph 3 refers to

(A) the races at Olympia
(B) the modern Olympic Games
(C) the crown of olive leaves
(D) the Ancient Olympic Games

4. All of the following are true of the Ancient Olympics EXCEPT

(A) only men took part
(B) athletes took part naked
(C) the prize was a gold medal
(D) it was held in the city of Olympia

5. Which of the following best expresses the essential information in the highlighted sentence? Incorrect answers change the meaning in important ways or leave out essential information.

There was much differentiation between the modern Olympics and the ancient Greek games.

(A) The modern Olympics did not differ too much from those of ancient times.
(B) There was only one change that occurred in the modern Olympics to make it different from the games of ancient Greece.
(C) There was a lot of arguing about what should make the new Olympics different from the ancient Greek games.
(D) There were many things that made the modern Olympic Games different from those held in ancient Greece.

6. Complete the table below by selecting the appropriate phrases from the answer choices and matching them to the correct heading. TWO of the answer choices will not be used. **This question is worth 4 points.**

(A) No women allowed
(B) Held in 767 BCE
(C) More than half the athletes women
(D) Naked athletes
(E) 240 athletes take part
(F) Athletes win medals for first time
(G) Professionals take part now
(H) Athletes win olive crown
(I) Nine different sport events

Ancient Olympics
- _____
- _____
- _____

1896 Athens Olympics
- _____
- _____

2004 Athens Olympics
- _____
- _____

Check-up

A. Choose the correct answer.

1. When answering a table question, you should
   (A) eliminate answer choices with information that is relevant to the categories in the chart.
   (B) eliminate answer choices with information that is not related to the passage.
   (C) eliminate answer choices with information that supports the main idea of the passage.
   (D) eliminate answer choices that include main ideas from the passage.

Key Vocabulary Practice

B. Fill in the blanks with the correct words.

whistles	musical	respected	scored	community halls
referee	goal posts	helmets	humorous	acting

1. British actor, Sir Laurence Olivier, practiced a style of _____ called "the Method."

2. _____ must know the rules of their sport better than anyone else.

3. In rugby, players can get points for drop kicks that land over the _____.

4. In some countries, policemen blow _____ when they chase criminals.

5. The Dalai Lama is a(n) _____ figure in the Buddhist world.

6. *The Phantom of the Opera* is a famous _____.

7. P.G. Wodehouse is well known for writing very _____ novels.

8. Cyclists that compete in the Tour de France race have to wear _____.

9. Most towns and cities have _____ where people meet up for events.

10. Brazil _____ two goals against Germany in the World Cup soccer final in 2002.

Shakespeare's Globe Theater

Few people know that William Shakespeare was a professional and very capable actor. He not only wrote many plays; he also acted in them. In 1599, he and some acting colleagues took the initiative to build a new theater in London. They called it the Globe. It was big enough for 3,000 people to assemble in.

The people of London in the sixteenth and early seventeenth century had a great appreciation for theater. They loved to come and watch Shakespeare and his friends do plays at the Globe. The actors would do their vocal exercises to warm up their voices. Then they would get into their costumes and the fun would begin. The audience used to scream and shout with joy. They were not quiet like today's theater audiences. If a play was very popular, the actors would have to do successive performances.

Shakespeare used to make up stories and turn them into plays. He also wrote adaptations of classical Greek and Roman stories. His versions of stories about Julius Caesar or Queen Cleopatra have become very famous. All these plays were put on at the Globe.

The Globe was an open-air theater and built out of wood. In 1613 it burnt down in a fire. Luckily, no one had any injuries from the fire. Shakespeare and his friends quickly decided to restore the theater. They did not want to abandon it because for them it was a very special place. They re-built it in June 1614. Shakespeare died in 1616 but the pace of performances did not slow down. There were always actors looking for work. The Globe stayed open and carried on.

In 1642, it was closed down by Oliver Cromwell, the leader of the Puritans. He was the new English ruler and believed theater was bad for people. He soon broke down the theater to build houses in its place.

In 1995, an American actor called Sam Wanamaker asked the British government to build a new Globe theater as the equivalent of the old one. He believed people all over the world would have appreciation for this. In 1997, the new Globe opened its doors.

Choose the correct answers.

1. All of the following are true about William Shakespeare EXCEPT

    (A) he was an actor

    (B) he did not write plays

    (C) he built the Globe theater with colleagues

    (D) he wrote adaptations of classical stories

2. The writer discusses the theater audiences of sixteenth and early seventeenth century London in order to

    (A) examine how much theater has changed in the last 500 years

    (B) show that Shakespeare built the Globe because theater was so popular

    (C) illustrate how badly behaved and noisy the audiences were

    (D) suggest that Shakespeare and his colleagues made a lot of money

3. In stating in paragraph 4 that Shakespeare and his friends did not want to abandon the Globe, the writer means that

    (A) they did not mean for it to burn down

    (B) they did not want to pay too much to rebuild it

    (C) they did not want to give up and desert the theater

    (D) they did not want to sell the Globe

4. What can be inferred from the last paragraph about Sam Wanamaker?

    (A) He wanted to be as famous as Shakespeare.

    (B) He wished he had lived in Shakespeare's time.

    (C) He wanted to restore the Globe for today's Shakespeare fans.

    (D) He thought that London was not the same without the Globe.

5. The phrase for this in the last paragraph refers to

    (A) the work of the British government

    (B) re-building the equivalent of the old Globe Theater

    (C) the request of Sam Wanamaker

    (D) the old Globe Theater of Shakespeare's time

6. Complete the table below by selecting the appropriate phrases from the answer choices and matching them to the correct person. TWO of the answer choices will not be used. **This question is worth 4 points.**

William Shakespeare

(A) Believed the world would like a new Globe
  • _____
(B) Closed the Globe theater in 1642
  • _____
(C) Died in 1642 and then Globe closed down
  • _____
(D) Opened the Globe theater in 1614

Oliver Cromwell
(E) Asked for re-building of equivalent of Globe
  • _____
(F) Broke Globe down to build houses
  • _____
(G) Restored the Globe in 1614

Sam Wanamaker
(H) Wrote adaptations of classics
  • _____
(I) Opened the Globe theater in 1599
  • _____

Sigmund Freud

Sigmund Freud was an Austrian brain doctor. He was born on May 6, 1856. Freud was very interested in human psychology. He decided to pursue a career as a psychologist. He had many hypotheses about how the human mind works and about human thoughts and feelings. Freud studied people with mind problems. He listened to what they spoke about and assessed their thoughts. Freud believed that having someone to listen to helped people deal with problems. By talking things out, people usually feel better. This idea has become known as "the talking cure." Today, psychologists still utilize it.

Many of Freud's patients were very tense. They did not know what caused their stress. Freud believed he could find the answers not only by listening to them but also in their dreams. He asked them to brainstorm and write down what they dreamed about. He believed this could trigger ideas about what was really wrong with them.

Freud believed that people hide their true feelings in their dreams. They sometimes have a reluctance to face their true feelings. He believed he could help people by showing them what their dreams meant. He could reveal the implications of their dreams.

In 1899, Freud published a book called *The Interpretation of Dreams*. All the chapters in this book were about his ideas. Many other mind doctors did not agree with Freud. They did not think that he was neutral about his patients. They believed he saw in them what he wanted to see. They also questioned his ethics. They did not think Freud could be trusted. They thought he just wanted to be famous. They questioned the validity of his dream hypothesis.

There were also many people who supported Freud. ■ 1) In 1930, he received a prize in appreciation of his work in the field of psychology. ■ 2) Today, there are many psychologists who think Freud was right about dreams. ■ 3) In the field of psychology, it is those who support Freud versus the doctors who don't think he was right. ■ 4) If you visit a psychologist, you can ask them if they are a Freudian. That means he or she supports Freud and his theories.

Choose the correct answers.

1. The word hypotheses in paragraph 1 is closest in meaning to
   (A) theories
   (B) ideas
   (C) suggestions
   (D) thoughts

2. The author uses "the talking cure" as an example of

   (A) an untested theory from psychology
   (B) a treatment method still used today
   (C) how Freud treated patients badly
   (D) Freud's hypotheses about the mind

3. Which of the following best expresses the essential information in the highlighted sentence? Incorrect answers change the meaning in important ways or leave out essential information.

   He believed this could trigger ideas about what was really wrong with them.

   (A) He imagined this might get their thoughts going about their main problems.
   (B) He guessed there was a chance this could lead to interesting concepts.
   (C) He thought this might cause them to think strange things.
   (D) He felt this would give them wrong ideas about their problems.

4. According to the passage, many other doctors did not think Freud could be trusted because

   (A) the chapters of his book were full of lies.
   (B) he wanted to win a prize for his book about psychology.
   (C) they thought he used his patients to become famous.
   (D) they believed he stole his dream hypothesis from another doctor.

5. Look at the four squares (■) that indicate where the following sentence could be added to the passage.

   In fact, he had many fans and followers who thought he was a great man.

   Where would the sentence best fit?

   (A) Square 1   (B) Square 2
   (C) Square 3   (D) Square 4

6. An introductory sentence for a brief summary of the passage is provided below. Complete the summary by selecting the THREE answer choices that express the most important ideas in the passage. Some sentences do not belong in the summary because they express ideas that are not presented in the passage or are minor ideas in the passage. **This question is worth 2 points.**

   Sigmund Freud was an Austrian psychologist with many controversial theories and ideas.

   (A) Others felt that Freud helped sick people a lot with his psychology treatments, and today many doctors still use his methods.
   (B) Freud believed that talking about feelings and thinking about the meaning of dreams could help people to cure their problems and stress.
   (C) Freudians are doctors who use Freud's methods not only on patients but also on themselves.
   (D) Freud felt that dreams sometimes contain the most truth because people often lie to themselves but dreams cannot lie.
   (E) Freud wrote a book about this, and some psychologists felt that Freud was using his patients to become famous.

The Fishing Industry

The world's fishing industry is in big trouble. This is because there is a high incidence of over-fishing. Fishing companies are extracting too many fish from our oceans. Greedy fishing companies exceed the amount of fish they may take out. They are also taking out under-sized fish. There is no distinction made between good-sized fish and fish that are too small to eat. By doing this the fish cannot breed. There are not enough mature fish to make babies. If this doesn't stop we could run out of fish.

Environmentalists have a lot to contend with. They want to stop fishing companies from over-fishing. Fishing needs to be minimized to offset the harm done by over-fishing. We need to restore fish stocks so that there is a good distribution of fish. There are no protocols in place to see that this gets done. There are no codes of conduct to protect the oceans. Every country has different laws about fishing. There is no integration when it comes to these laws.

For example, many countries have laws against killing whales. They believe that whaling is bad. Whaling is done in Japan because Japanese people do not think it is so bad. Japan has different laws about whaling from other countries. They have a different culture about whaling too.

At a conference held in 2006, the International Whaling Commission (IWC) talked about this problem. ■ 1) They agreed that Japan could start whaling again when there were enough whales in the sea. ■ 2) Japanese fishermen did not want to wait. ■ 3) They kept on killing and hunting whales in secret. ■ 4) Many people are very angry about that.

The principle of protecting the fish and other animals that live in our oceans is a good one. If we take out too many fish, soon there will be none left. Another problem is pollutants from our factories that kill fish. Fish that feed on tiny micro-organisms near the surface of the sea often get poisoned. If we eat too much of these fish, we can get sick too.

Choose the correct answers.

1. The word distinction in paragraph 1 is closest in meaning to
(A) dedication
(B) direction
(C) difference
(D) differentiation

2. According to paragraph 1, the fishing industry is in trouble mainly because
(A) people all over the world are greedy and eat too many fish
(B) there is a high incidence of over-eating fish that eat other fish
(C) fishing companies are taking out too many under-sized fish
(D) fish can no longer breed because they have become too small

3. Which of the following best expresses the essential information in the highlighted sentence? Incorrect answers change the meaning in important ways or leave out essential information.

   Fishing needs to be minimized to offset the harm done by over-fishing.

   (A) Fish extraction needs to be halted to make sure no fish are in danger.
   (B) There should be less fishing to balance the damage caused by too much fishing.
   (C) Fishing must be stopped or else those that over-fish may be hurt.
   (D) Lessening the amount of fishing done cannot alter the injuries done to fish.

4. What can be inferred about the writer's attitude to Japanese whale hunting?

   (A) He seems against it.
   (B) He seems to support it.
   (C) He seems to be neutral.
   (D) He seems undecided.

5. Look at the four squares (■) that indicate where the following sentence could be added to the passage.

   They decided not to listen to the IWC.

   Where would the sentence best fit?

   (A) Square 1   (B) Square 2
   (C) Square 3   (D) Square 4

6. An introductory sentence for a brief summary of the passage is provided below. Complete the summary by selecting the THREE answer choices that express the most important ideas in the passage. Some sentences do not belong in the summary because they express ideas that are not presented in the passage or are minor ideas in the passage. **This question is worth 2 points.**

   Over-fishing by greedy fishing companies is a big problem.

   (A) With other problems like pollution also hurting fish, it is important that we start doing something to save the fish.
   (B) The problem is that there are no rules and laws in the world to protect the fish and governments do not agree about what to do.
   (C) Environmentalists are angry with fishing companies that steal fish and kill whales in Japan.
   (D) Japanese people don't think whaling is bad but other people do, and this causes fighting.
   (E) It means that fish may run out if we don't minimize fishing because fish cannot breed enough.

Basic Skills for the
TOEFL® iBT 3

Moraig Macgillivray
Kayang Gagiano

Reading

Transcript & Answer Key

Answer Key

[Unit 1]

Getting Ready

Page 8

C

4, 2, 1, 3

D

Topic: Women in the Military

General history: Today — OK for women to serve in the military. Women used to be forbidden from fighting.

Example: The first woman in the American military was Deborah Sampson in 1782. Pretended to be a man. Was discovered by a doctor.

Women's status: Women have worked hard to be seen as equals. Militaries don't want women to fight because of risk. Laws were often made to protect women. Not all women conform to people's ideas of how they should act.

Opposition: Some think that women are physically weaker than men are. Others say that some women are strong enough. Standards should be the same for men and women.

Page 9

E

1. A   2. A   3. B   4. A

F

1. conform   2. risk   3. undergo
4. opposed   5. forbidden

Practice

Page 11

C

1. B   2. B   3. B   4. A

D

1. labor   2. exploited   3. expose
4. displaced   5. integrity

Test

Page 12

1. A   2. C   3. B   4. A
5. C   6. A, C, D

Check-up

Page 14

A

1. A   2. B

B

1. equal   2. battle   3. collapse
4. frail   5. settlers   6. dainty
7. acceptable 8. treaty   9. tribe
10. dependent

[Unit 2]

Getting Ready

Page 16

C

5, 4, 2, 3, 1

D

Topic: Nineteenth Century Photography

Introduction: Nineteenth century photography in the US saw enormous advances. We can learn about history. We can learn about the art of photography.

Daguerreotype: Used a silver-plated sheet, like a mirror. Exposed to image from inside the camera. Final image was sharp.

Ambrotype: Used from 1854 to the early 1860s. Popular because it was cheaper. Used one glass plate to expose image and another to protect it. Final image inserted into a frame.

Tintype:	Used a thin, black, <u>metal plate</u>. Invented in <u>1856</u> and popular until <u>early 1900s</u>. Weren't as <u>fragile</u> as ambrotypes.

Page 17

E

1. B   2. A   3. B   4. A

F

1. precedes   2. enormous   3. infer
4. insert   5. attached

Practice

Page 19

C

1. A   2. B   3. A   4. B

D

1. founded   2. invoke   3. scenarios
4. adjacent   5. diversity

Test

Page 20

1. C   2. C   3. D
4. B   5. A
6.

Visual Art
• (D) Photography
• (E) Computer graphics
• (F) Sculpture

Other Art
• (A) Music
• (G) Literature

Check-up

Page 22

A

1. C   2. B

B

1. shackles   2. photography   3. oppressed
4. subject   5. fled   6. sharp
7. expose   8. visual   9. liberty
10. frame

[Unit 3]

Getting Ready

Page 24

C

4, 2, 1, 5, 3

D

Topic:	<u>Life Science</u>
What it is:	The study of all <u>living things</u>: animals, <u>humans</u>, and plants. Also of <u>micro-organisms</u>.
Other name:	<u>Biology</u>, comes from <u>two Greek words</u>. Many <u>scientific</u> words are Greek because they studied <u>nature first</u>.
Aristotle:	Greek <u>philosopher</u>, lived <u>from 384 BCE to 322 BCE</u>. Known as <u>father of biology</u>. One of <u>first</u> people to make very <u>accurate</u> studies of <u>plants and animals</u>.
His methods:	Had a lot of <u>perseverance</u>. Studied each animal for a long <u>time</u> to get to <u>know it</u>.
His beliefs:	Scientists have to be <u>rigorous</u>, can't take <u>any guesses</u>. Didn't <u>confine</u> his studies. He <u>traveled</u> a lot. Many of his <u>methods</u> still used today.

Page 25

E

1. B   2. B   3. A   4. A

F

1. Rigorous   2. accurate   3. biology
4. perseverance   5. confined

Practice

Page 27

C

1. B   2. A   3. A   4. B

D

1. prohibit   2. controversial   3. evolution
4. colleagues 5. incompatible

Test

Page 28

1. A   2. B   3. C
4. D   5. D   6. C, A, D

Check-up

Page 30

A

1. B   2. A

B

1. Bible   2. ignore   3. experiments
4. origin   5. species   6. evil
7. philosopher 8. microscopes   9. scientific
10. micro-organisms

[Unit 4]

Getting Ready

Page 32

C

2, 5, 1, 3, 4

D

Topic:	Sleep
Introduction:	All human beings need sleep to live. Enough sleep is integral to health. During the sleeping hours our bodies rest and repair themselves. Studies show that people who get less sleep often die younger.
Sleeping problems:	Many people struggle to sleep well. They experience fluctuations in their sleeping patterns. Wake up in the middle of the night a lot. Feel tired and lack energy.
Studies:	Doctors and scientists have studied sleeping problems. Found that people with lots of stress at work or who don't exercise enough have trouble sleeping.
Medication:	Doctors sometimes give patients sleeping aids. Can include medication such as sleeping pills.
Other solutions:	Use vitamins or food supplements. Eating well and exercising. Drinking something warm before bedtime. Don't eat a heavy meal.

Page 33

E

1. A   2. B   3. A   4. A

F

1. fluctuations   2. supplements   3. ultimately
4. aid   5. integral

Practice

Page 35

C

1. B   2. B   3. A   4. A

D

1. conceive   2. defect   3. mature
4. induce   5. utilized

Test

Page 36

1. D   2. A   3. C
4. C   5. B

6.

Healthy adult heart

- (B) Beats seventy-two times in one minute
- (E) Weighs between 250 and 350 grams

Sick adult heart

- (A) Enlarged, weighs up to one kilogram
- (C) Needs medication to stop heart attack
- (F) Heartbeat fluctuates and need pacemaker

Check-up

Page 38

A

1. B   2. D

B

1. lack   2. pregnant   3. blood pressure
4. addicted   5. melatonin   6. patients
7. sonar   8. fertile   9. heartbeats
10. medication

[Unit 5]

Getting Ready

Page 40

C

2, 1, 4, 3

D

Topic:	Effective Management and the Employee Interview
Importance of leadership:	Managers have to make sure the business is <u>running well</u>. Have to make sure workers are <u>doing their best</u>. Need to be good <u>leaders</u>.
How to lead:	Should understand what makes people <u>work</u>. Must provide <u>motivation</u>. Workers want to feel <u>appreciated</u>.
Interviews:	Interviews can improve <u>worker–manager relations</u>. Chance to <u>compile</u> information. Workers can <u>express</u> their attitudes and feel like they are <u>being listened to</u>. Workers are more likely to be <u>cooperative</u>.
Employee understanding:	Workers should know the <u>interview's purpose</u>. They shouldn't think it is an <u>evaluation or they'll perform differently</u>. If they see it as a chance to express themselves it will be <u>more productive</u>.

Page 41

E

1. D   2. A

F

1. enhance   2. compiled   3. termination
4. cooperative 5. motivation

Practice

Page 43

C

1. B   2. B   3. B   4. D

D

1. insights   2. commodities 3. coincides
4. aggregate   5. inclination

Test

Page 44

1. A   2. B   3. A
4. D   5. C   6. A, B, D

Check-up

Page 46

A

1. A

B

1. x-axis   2. productive   3. brief
4. y-axis   5. manager   6. appreciate
7. demand   8. relations   9. Supply
10. intersection

[Unit 6]

Getting Ready

Page 48

C

4, 5, 2, 1, 3

D

Topic:	<u>Francois Péron</u>
Introduction:	<u>Anthropology</u> is the study of <u>human cultures</u>.
Francois Péron:	French <u>explorer</u>, first to use this word. <u>Undertook</u> a trip to <u>Australia</u> with scientists in <u>1801</u>. Wanted to learn about <u>indigenous people</u>. Also visited island of <u>Tasmania</u>. Met <u>Aborigines</u>.
Aborigines:	Big <u>tribe</u> who lived a <u>simple</u> life. Hunted <u>animals</u>, fished, and grew <u>vegetables</u>. Lived in <u>huts</u>, wore few <u>clothes</u>, spoke a strange <u>language</u>. Liked to tell <u>stories</u> round big <u>fire</u>, make <u>music</u> and art.
Péron's studies:	Studied Aborigine's <u>way of life</u> and <u>wrote</u> down everything. Knew most <u>Europeans</u> would think they were <u>uncivilized</u>. He thought <u>conduct</u> was interesting and culture <u>simple but not bad</u>.
Péron's wish:	Wanted Europeans to see that the <u>world</u> is full of people with <u>different</u> cultures, so made up <u>new word to study culture</u>.

Page 49

E

1. C, A, E   2. A   3. B   4. A

F

1. indigenous   2. conduct   3. uncivilized
4. undertook   5. definition

Practice

Page 51

C

1. C, E, B   2. B   3. A   4. A

D

1. contemporary   2. gender   3. persistent
4. rank   5. feminist

Test

Page 52

1. A   2. B   3. D
4. B   5. B   6. C, A, E

Check-up

Page 54

A

1. D

B

1. anthropology   2. way of life
3. married   4. marches
5. suffragette   6. wedding
7. explorer   8. raised
9. huts   10. Aborigines

[Review 1]

Reading 1

Page 55

1. D   2. C   3. B   4. B
5. C   6. D, A, C

Reading 2

Page 57

1. A   2. C   3. B   4. B
5. D   6. D, B, C

Answer Key

Reading 3

Page 59

1. C   2. A   3. D
4. A   5. D
6.

The World Bank 1945–1960

- (A) Loaned $250 million to France
- (D) Founding coincided with war end
- (F) Helped re-build post war Europe

The World Bank after 1960

- (B) Loans funds to fight diseases like HIV
- (E) Decided to help countries outside Europe

[Unit 7]

Getting Ready

Page 62

C

3, 1, 2, 5, 4

D

Topic:	Writing Novels
As career:	Pursuing one is not always easy. Writing novels can be a long process. Think of a good concept and storyline. Let your mind run free and write down every idea.
Novel structure:	Divide into chapters to give structure to the book. Develop your plot. Should have a good pace to excite your reader.
Readers:	Try to capture their imagination from very first page. Without action, readers may get bored.
Storyline:	Don't have too many storylines as it may confuse your reader. Better to start with a simple story and then develop it. Easier to add to a story than to take away!
Characters:	Develop your characters well and describe the way they look and think. Should seem like real people.

Page 63

E

1. A   2. B   3. B   4. A

F

1. pursued   2. brainstorm   3. pace
4. chapters   5. concepts

Practice

Page 65

C

1. A   2. B   3. B   4. B

D

1. prospect   2. allocations   3. drama
4. media   5. journalists

Test

Page 66

1. C   2. B   3. C
4. C   5. C   6. D, A, C

Check-up

Page 68

A

1. C   2. D

B

1. imagination   2. storyline   3. real
4. fiction   5. captured   6. Awards
7. prizes   8. newspapers   9. run free
10. press

[Unit 8]

Getting Ready

Page 70

C

3, 1, 2

D

Topic:	Geothermal Heating
Problems with fossil fuels:	Fossil fuels pollute the air. Fossil fuels are non-renewable so they can't be restored. Fossil fuels are expensive like all scarce resources.
Geothermal heating:	The Earth is a natural source of heat. We can extract heat by putting a heat pump deep in the Earth. It is a clean energy source and it never runs out.
Financial considerations:	Need to have another source of heat. Using geothermal as your principle heat source will save money. Geothermal heating systems are expensive to install. Geothermal heating systems save money in the long-run.

Page 71

E

1. B   2. B   3. A   4. A

F

1. principle   2. extract   3. incentive
4. pollutants   5. restore

Practice

Page 73

C

1. A   2. B   3. B   4. A

D

1. offset   2. minimize   3. implications
4. assess   5. exceed

Test

Page 74

1. C   2. D   3. B
4. C   5. A
6.

Point-source pollution

- (A) Factories
- (C) Farms
- (G) Oil spills

Non-point-source pollution

- (E) General garbage
- (F) Various contaminants from water sports and commercial boating

Check-up

Page 76

A

1. C   2. B

B

1. Greenhouse gases
2. grasp   3. counter   4. comfortable
5. long run   6. Geothermal 7. consumption
8. non-renewable 9. carbon footprint
10. dependence

[Unit 9]

Getting Ready

Page 78

C

2, 1, 4, 3

D

Topic:	The Effects of Smoking
Introduction:	Smoking is bad for your health. Diseases of the respiratory system are triggered by smoking. Also bad for the heart, brain, and for blood circulation.

Answer Key

Second-hand smoke:	Is bad, too. Children of smokers have <u>higher incidence of respiratory problems</u>. Children of smokers <u>don't perform as well in school</u>.
What to do:	People <u>shouldn't start</u> smoking. Smokers <u>should quit</u>. Though smoking is <u>decreasing</u>, people still smoke.
Why people smoke:	Smoking is hard to quit <u>because it is addictive</u>. Smokers think that <u>smoking relaxes them</u>, but <u>it's a stimulant</u>.

Page 79

E

1. A   2. B

F

1. incidence   2. reluctance   3. tense
4. triggered   5. Exposure

Practice

Page 81

C

1. A   2. B   3. A   4. B

D

1. psychology   2. validity   3. hypothesis
4. ethics   5. code

Test

Page 82

1. B   2. D   3. C
4. D   5. A   6. C, D, E

Check-up

Page 84

A

1. B   2. C

B

1. prevalence   2. addictive   3. Psychiatrists
4. applied   5. circulation 6. Respiratory
7. stimulant   8. therapy   9. bound
10. abused

[Unit 10]

Getting Ready

Page 86

C

2, 1, 4, 5, 3

D

Topic:	<u>E-books</u>
Space-saving advantage:	Can store <u>hundreds of books</u> in one e-book. Don't need <u>bookshelves for storage</u>.
Time-saving advantage:	E-books have same <u>functions as computers</u>. Can <u>search for certain words</u>. Can access other <u>texts through links</u>.
Accessibility advantage:	Readers with difficulty reading can <u>change text size</u>. Can also use software that <u>allows you to listen rather than read</u>.
Distribution advantage:	Easier for <u>publishers to distribute</u>. Books are <u>easy to replicate</u> and don't require <u>paper and ink</u>. Books can <u>be sent electronically</u>.

Page 87

E

1. B   2. B   3. B   4. B

F

1. equivalent   2. version   3. Distribution
4. distinction   5. capable

Practice

Page 89

C

1. B   2. A   3. B

D

1. transport 2. marginal 3. Corporate
4. previous 5. items

Page 90

1. D 2. B 3. A
4. D 5. C
6.

Wi-Fi

- (A) Became available in 1997
- (F) Makes business more efficient
- (G) Requires industry standards

Cabled connection

- (B) Costly to install
- (D) Older technology

Check-up

Page 92

A

1. A 2. C

B

1. electronically 2. media
3. publishers 4. biodegradable
5. toxic 6. eco-friendly
7. links 8. upgrade
9. text 10. motherboard

[Unit 11]

Getting Ready

Page 94

C

3, 1, 5, 2, 4

D

Topic: Refugees
Introduction: Refugees are people who leave
their home country because they
are oppressed. Stay and may be
thrown in prison or killed.

Leaving: Have to abandon their homes,
jobs, and families and run away to
a new country.
Reasons: Usually because governments don't
like their politics or religion.
Integration: Not easy and life can be distressing
because refugees have lot to
contend with. Have to find home
and work and often no money.
Had to leave home urgently and
had no time to plan.
Governments: Problem is they think refugees are
not in danger. They think refugees
moved for convenience because
own country is poor. Believe they
seek better life in a rich country.

Page 95

E

1. D 2. A 3. A 4. A

F

1. politics 2. contend 3. convenience
4. integration 5. abandoned

Practice

Page 97

C

1. C 2. B 3. A 4. A

D

1. Successive 2. conferences 3. assembled
4. protocols 5. vocal

Test

Page 98

1. B 2. A 3. B
4. B 5. C 6. E, A, C

Answer Key

Check-up

Page 100

A

1. A

B

1. refugees   2. urgently   3. prison
4. distressing 5. environmental 6. flood
7. halt   8. Kyoto Protocol 9. oppressed
10. Global warming

[Unit 12]

Getting Ready

Page 102

C

4, 3, 1, 2

D

Topic:	Amateur Theater Groups
Introduction:	Amateur theater is popular in many countries. Unlike professional theater, no one gets paid. People do it because they have great appreciation for theater and a love of acting. Great way to make friends and fun for whole family.
Where they meet:	Amateur groups usually meet in a school or community hall. Professional actors meet in real theaters and live and work in big cities.
The Plays:	Amateurs usually do classical plays or those by famous and respected writers. Often choose humorous plays, adaptations, or musicals. Professionals do new plays by exciting writers and more serious plays.

How often:	Amateurs usually do one or two plays a year. Only meet after work or on weekends. Professionals try to do more plays.

Page 103

E

1.

Amateur Theater

- (A) Often choose musicals or funny plays
- (E) Act for fun and appreciation
- (G) In community halls or schools

Professional Actors

- (B) Meet in real theaters in big cities
- (C) Get paid to act
- (F) Often do new plays by exciting writers
- (H) Do more plays to make more money

2. B

F

1. professional   2. appreciation   3. adaptations
4. amateurs   5. classical

Practice

Page 105

C

1.

American Football

- (A) Uses an oval-shaped ball
- (B) Points scored with touchdowns

Soccer

- (F) Played without helmets
- (H) Points scored by goal in net
- (I) Called football in England

Both sports

- (C) Uses a referee
- (D) Played with eleven players

2. B

D

1. uniforms   2. differentiation   3. versus
4. injuries   5. neutral

Page 106

1. A   2. B   3. D
4. C   5. D
6.

Ancient Olympics

• (A) No women allowed
• (D) Naked athletes
• (H) Athletes win olive crown

1896 Athens Olympics

• (F) Athletes win medals for first time
• (I) Nine different sport events

2004 Athens Olympics

• (C) More than half the athletes women
• (G) Professionals take part now

Check-up

Page 108

A

1. B

B

1. acting   2. Referees   3. goal posts
4. whistles   5. respected   6. musical
7. humorous   8. helmets   9. community halls
10. scored

[Review 2]

Reading 1

Page 109

1. B   2. B   3. C
4. C   5. B
6.

William Shakespeare

• (D) Opened the Globe theater in 1599
• (G) Restored the Globe in 1614
• (H) Wrote adaptations of classics

Oliver Cromwell

• (B) Closed the Globe theater in 1642
• (F) Broke Globe down to build houses

Sam Wanamaker

• (A) Believed the world would like a new Globe
• (E) Asked for re-building of equivalent of Globe

Reading 2

Page 111

1. A   2. B   3. A   4. C
5. A   6. B, E, A

Reading 3

Page 113

1. D   2. C   3. B
4. C   5. C   6. E, B, A